MUSTANG 5.0

PERFORMANCE PROJECTS

MUSTANG 5.0

PERFORMANCE PROJECTS

HUW EVANS

MOTORBOOKS
INTERNATIONAL

Dedication

I would like to dedicate this book to my Mom and Dad, brother Owain,
and also to my significant other, Andrea, for their wisdom and tremendous encouragement over the years.
Without it, I probably wouldn't have entered the fray of automotive journalism
nor written this book. Here's to you!

First published in 2004 by Motorbooks International, an imprint of MBI Publishing Company, Galtier Plaza, Suite 200, 380 Jackson Street, St. Paul, MN 55101-3885 USA.

The information in this book is true and complete to the best of our knowledge. All recommendations are made without any guarantee on the part of the author or Publisher, who also disclaim any liability incurred in connection with the use of this data or specific details.

This publication has been prepared solely by MBI Publishing Company and is not approved or licensed by any other entity. We recognize that some words, model names and designation mentioned herein are the property of the trademark holder. We use them for identification purposes only. This is not an official publication.

Motorbooks International titles are also available at discounts in bulk quantity for industrial or sales-promotional use. For details write to the Special Sales Manager at Motorbooks International Wholesalers & Distributors, Galtier Plaza, Suite 200, 380 Jackson Street, St. Paul, MN 55101-3885 USA.

Front cover: photos courtesy Jerry Heasley (main), David Newhardt, and Huw Evans (insets)

On the frontis and Title page: *David Newhardt*

On the back cover: *David Newhardt*

About the Author: Huw Evans was born in Wales and currently lives near Toronto, Ontario, Canada. A life-long car nut, Huw loves just about anything automotive, though he does have a soft spot for Mustangs and currently owns a 1986 GT. His passion for Ford's original pony car first got him into the realm of automotive journalism and ultimately lured him across the Atlantic. He is the former editor of *Hot Cars* and currently freelances for *High Performance Pontiac, Muscle Car Enthusiast, Mustang Enthusiast,* and *Classic American*. Cars aside, Huw's other passion is video games. His previous book is *The Cars of Gran Turismo*.

ISBN 0-7603-1545-0

Edited by Lindsay Hitch
Layout by Brenda Canales

Printed in China

Contents

Acknowledgments

Although my name appears on the front, this book is entirely a collaborative effort, and without the help of a number of individuals, *Mustang 5.0 Performance Projects* probably wouldn't be in your hands today. First, I would like to extend a tremendous thank you to Joe Da Silva and his crew at Da Silva Racing in Scarborough, Ontario, Canada—Diago, Fab, Josh, and Murray. Joe is the quintessential professional and has built up one of the foremost late-model Mustang shops in North America. Joe has always been there whenever I've needed advice or servicing regarding my own 5-liter Mustang and has always gone out of his way to accommodate me. He also gave unparalleled access to anything I needed when taking photographs and compiling copy for this book. Thanks, Joe—I owe you one!

I would also like to thank Evan Smith of *Muscle Mustangs and Fast Fords* for supplying me with photography when needed and really helping speed up the process of putting this book together; Jerry Heasley for supplying the great cover photography; Tim Weir and Vanessa Van Dette, two of the most diehard Ford and Mustang fanatics I've ever met, who have since become great friends, for helping set up some of the projects for this book; Peter Buckley at Donway Ford Collision Center in Toronto for his amazing bumper repair work; Lawrence Chamberlin for allowing me to use his 1995 GT for the convertible top project; Harold and Terry at New Image Interiors, Scarborough, Ontario; Ken Britt for helping with the head and intake upgrades; Mark Hughes for putting me in touch with Motorbooks International; and finally to the editors at MBI who got me involved with this book and helped keep it on the rails, Lee Klancher and Peter Bodensteiner—thanks a lot, guys!

—*Huw Evans*
Barrie, Ontario, Canada

Introduction

Automotive performance in North America took a huge nosedive after the early 1970s, with the onset of the energy crisis and fuel economy and emissions mandates. It seemed that sporty domestic cars would be relics of the past. Then, in the early 1980s, things began to change.

At the forefront of this Detroit renaissance in performance was the 5-liter Ford Mustang. At the time, few people could envision that this one car, as potent as it was for the era, could emerge to become a household name on the street. Thanks to its virtually unbeatable bang for the buck and simplicity, the 5-liter became a bona fide king of the street and remained so, despite the debut of more sophisticated rivals from other manufacturers—virtually none of which could match it in performance, charisma, and, especially, price.

Hot rodders soon discovered that not only was the newest Mustang a great performer in factory guise but that the 5-liter High Output V-8 underhood responded to performance modification as a cat does to milk. Enthusiasts were able to coax tremendous speed and power from the car at relatively little cost. Even a decade after the debut of that first 1982 GT, these Mustangs (stock or modified) were still the benchmark for affordable performance. So popular did this humble pony become for modification (particularly the fuel-injected 1986–1993 versions) that it led to the creation of one of the largest performance aftermarket industries tailored to a single car.

The 5-liter was popular not only from an enthusiast standpoint but from a commercial one. The original Fox-chassis Mustang debuted as a 1979 model, and the same underpinnings were still being used on the 2004 model, meaning that this platform has served in Mustangs for over a quarter century.

Today, these attributes still make this car one of the best performance buys on the market. Supply is fairly plentiful, and the production longevity of the hardware means that pieces designed for later cars retrofit older Mustangs with few problems. Furthermore, enthusiast following and aftermarket support is stronger than ever. It can be truthfully said that the 5-liter Mustang embodies the American dream more than any other car of recent times. It offers decent performance and the ability to build a unique ride at a price almost anybody can afford. Interest in the Fox and SN95 5-liters, to quote a recent Ford promotion, knows "no boundaries," and people from all different backgrounds are united in their passion for these cars.

For all its wonderful attributes, the 5-liter Mustang can be improved in many ways—looks, performance, and handling—through maintenance and modification. *Mustang 5.0 Performance Projects* provides enthusiasts and followers of third- and fourth- generation 5-liter ponies with a selection of projects they can tackle to improve their Mustangs.

Not surprisingly considering the car's popularity, many reference sources—some better than others—have been devoted over the years to working on 5-liters. This book can't cover every aspect of working on and upgrading these cars, but I have attempted to provide a selection of some of the more useful and beneficial projects you can carry out, while attempting to separate some of the myths from the facts concerning these cars.

Recognizing that the vast majority of 5-liter Mustangs are still street driven, I've geared each project toward a regularly driven car that will occasionally see race duty. However, some experienced Mustang racers have contributed information that can translate into significant improvements for your street pony.

The projects have been grouped under specific areas—engine, transmission and rear end, chassis, brakes, suspension, exterior, and interior. Each project incorporates a legend illustrating the difficulty level (on a scale of 1–5), and also the tools, time required, and the likely overall cost. References to "right" and "left" sides of the car mean as viewed from the driver's seat. For some of the larger projects, such as selecting the right cylinder heads, automatic transmission upgrades, and installing a supercharger, you may benefit from the help of an experienced mechanic or performance shop. The information I've included in those instances should help you make informed decisions.

Even if this is the first book you purchase that's tailored to 5-liter Ford ponies, it shouldn't be the only one in your collection. It's meant to complement other manuals and technical reference books for these cars, a selection of which is listed at the back. *Mustang 5.0 Performance Projects* has also been designed so that you can pick out certain sections at your leisure, because few owners are likely to perform the projects in the order listed.

Although the 5-liter is a fairly simple car to work on, safety and patience are of paramount importance. A little common sense goes a long way in providing the utmost in satisfaction and enjoyment from your Mustang. If something doesn't seem right, use your head—it will save you a great deal of frustration, pain, and injury in the long run.

I have always wanted to write a book on 5-liter Mustangs, and this work has been a great learning experience, not to mention tremendous fun. I hope you get as much entertainment and satisfaction from it as I have. Enjoy!

Tools and Safety

Given the age and popularity of most 5-liter Mustangs, botched repairs are common. Most of the time, they were carried out without proper tools. Tools of good quality and in good condition are essential to achieving successful results.

Basic Tools

Even if you have limited experience working on your Mustang and are likely to carry out only basic upgrades and repairs, a good-quality basic tool set is essential. While a complete line of Snap-on tools is beyond the scope of most people, you can still purchase good-quality tools for a fairly reasonable cash outlay. Probably the best bet is to buy Craftsman tools from Sears, or Husky brand items, usually found at The Home Depot. Both of these are good quality, American-made tools. Both manufacturers offer almost unparalleled warranties—no matter what you've done to a tool, you can return it and they'll replace it, free. Cheaper tools may seem like a bargain, but they're made of lower-cost steel and will suffer damage, break more easily, and will likely not be guaranteed.

Unless you have a big tool budget, buy a basic set of tools to get started, then add to it as you discover what additional tools you need. If you keep your tools clean and in their place, they'll always be available when you need them.

Screwdrivers

You'll need several sizes of Phillips and flat-blade screwdrivers. Make sure the tips are in good shape, because a damaged screwdriver will easily strip and damage the head of a screw. A ratcheting screwdriver is a good idea for pulling out stubborn screws. Also handy is a Craftsman damaged-screw remover.

Wrenches

Fundamental to any quality tool kit are decent combination wrenches—one side open-ended, the other box-ended (closed like a circle). The 5-liter Mustang, like most Detroit cars of its era, contains both standard and metric fasteners, so you'll need combination wrenches in both sizes.

Allen or Hex Key Wrenches

These always come in handy. At the very least, make sure you have a basic set, though if you're building a tool arsenal and are into performing more complex repairs, Allen socket drivers and T-handles can be useful too. The socket drivers fit on the end of a ratchet and are great when you need to apply extra torque. Because you can also use them with extenders, they can be convenient in tight spaces.

Torque Wrenches

The clickety-click sound of a torque socket goes hand-in-hand with home auto maintenance and repairs. Probably no single tool is as useful or important as a good-quality torque wrench. You'll need to obtain a torque wrench that has both Imperial and metric measurements. Ideally buy two, one for smaller jobs (0–25 ft-lb is often recommended) and a bigger one for anything that requires more torque.

Adjustable Wrench

Sometimes called Crescent wrenches (the name of the original manufacturer), these are helpful when it comes to removing really tough or rusted larger nuts and bolts, which you'll no doubt come across on the majority of 5-liter Mustangs. Make sure you buy the best one you can afford, because poor-quality adjustables will damage the bolt heads and are more trouble than they're worth.

Pliers

Buy pliers whose teeth will stay sharp. Cheap pliers often burr after a couple of uses and are then worthless. You should have adjustable, needlenose, and Channelloks (a type of locking pliers) in your toolbox.

Sockets

Many mechanics have discovered that six-point sockets last longer than twelve-pointers and don't do as much damage to fasteners. You'll also need to purchase regular and deep sockets, and Torx sockets as well. The most common drive sizes are 1/4-, 3/8-, and 1/2-inch. You'll probably find 3/8 the most useful on your Mustang (and on any car or light truck). Start off with a small set rather than buying them individually, and get a good-quality ratchet.

Timing Light

Adjusting ignition timing is one of the most popular 5-liter tuning tricks, and Sears is a good source for them. Ideally you want a timing light with degree adjustability. This enables you to fine-tune ignition timing without relying on the timing marks on the crank (if they're still there), as is necessary with standard, nonadjustable timing lights.

Hammers

Especially when dealing with heavy items, such as the front spindles and tie rod ends, you need a good hammer. You'll probably want a soft-blow hammer and a middleweight ball-peen hammer, such as a 16-ouncer, for removing things like the heads and intake.

Fluorescent Shop Lamp

These lamps are usually available with or without a spring-loaded cable that winds back into the main housing. Either is good, though the winding type is particularly good for illuminating tight areas. Don't use lamps with standard 60-watt bulbs for working on your car, because they get hot and are a potential safety and fire hazard.

Wire Brush

A copper wire brush enables you to remove old gasket material effectively, without damaging the surface beneath it.

Automotive Scraper

This is handy when scraping excess material, including thick old gaskets and general grunge.

Tubing Cutter

If you're performing brake upgrades, you'll probably have to replace the fittings on your original brake lines. A tubing cutter lets you make a clean cut to pull off the old line nuts.

Miscellaneous

Items that fall under this category include a good craft knife, scissors, industrial tape, a measuring tape, steel files, shop towels (great for cleaning hands and wiping up spills), and an inspection mirror for looking into tight crevices.

Advanced Tools

Although this book is intended more for the Mustang hobbyist than speed-shop mechanics, you'll still need a couple of advanced tools to complete the projects.

Flare Fitting Wrenches

When you're into more complex tasks, such as swapping brake line nuts, flare fitting wrenches are essential to properly cut and make double flares for the brake lines.

Feeler Gauge

A feeler gauge, for gapping spark plugs, is an indispensable part of any mechanic or enthusiast's tool collection.

Clutch Alignment Tool

This is essential for properly centering your clutch disc and for making sure that the input shaft of a manual transmission can be properly mated to the pilot bearing. You'll need to buy a tool specific to your Mustang.

Breaker Bar

A breaker bar comes in handy with big, rusted bolts, including rusted-on lug nuts. This tool is also useful when you remove the distributor prior to pulling off your intake.

Puller

Sometimes you'll need to use a puller to remove items without damaging them, such as the pilot bearing in the clutch assembly. Pullers are widely available at auto parts stores and can often be rented.

Spring Compressor

One of the most hazardous jobs on the 5-liter Mustang (or any car) is removing the springs. Installing a compressor on the front springs, especially, enables you to relieve pressure before carefully removing them. This also reduces the risk of a tensioned spring popping out and causing serious harm.

Information Boxes–What They Mean

Time: An estimate of how long the project will take, based on an individual who has basic car and tool skills. If you don't know your timing light from an Allen wrench, you'll probably want to add time to this estimate.

Tools: What you need to do the job. For basic projects, all the tools are listed by size and type. For more complex projects, tools are listed by general category and combinations but not by size. Specialty tools are always listed separately and specifically.

Talent: Some projects require more skill than others. One star means the project can be completed by almost anyone with a desire to get dirty, while two stars means the project requires greater skill and knowledge. Projects that list four or five stars should be attempted only by those with advanced skills or left to a professional shop.

Applicable years: Some projects apply to certain years and models. Model and year are listed where appropriate. If no specific models years are mentioned, the project is suitable for all 5-liters.

Parts: The parts you'll need before embarking on the project.

Tab: The essence of the 5-liter Mustang (and of this book) is affordability, so a basic cost guide for parts (and labor in certain cases) is helpful. The prices shown are ballpark U.S. dollar figures, to help you when shopping for parts or expertise, and should be used as a rough guide, not an exact figure.

Tip: An insight to make the project easier. Often the tip can be learned only from working on these cars and is not found in the shop manual.

Performance Improvement: The benefits obtained from the project–for example, in handling, efficiency, or power. Sometimes they're obvious; sometimes not.

Complementary Project: Additional, related changes or modifications that add performance or other benefits.

SECTION 1

THE BASICS
Projects 1–3

PROJECT 1 ★ *Jacking Up Your Mustang*

Time: 20 minutes

Tools: 2-ton jack, axle stands

Talent: ★

Applicable years: All

Parts: None

Tab: $0

Tip: Make sure the car is firmly supported once it's on the axle stands.

Performance Improvement: The foundation for nearly every project.

One of the most important things when performing repairs or upgrades on your Mustang is to make sure the car is secure before working on it. Because most of the projects in this book require jacking up the vehicle, make sure you do this properly. A lift is the best and most convenient way. If you don't have access to one, use a hydraulic floor jack and secure the vehicle on axle stands.

Never work on the vehicle with just the jack underneath it, and don't rely on the factory jack for mechanical work. This jack is designed to raise only a part of the car, to allow you to change a tire. Only when one end or both ends of the car are raised and sitting level and secure should anyone ever crawl beneath your Mustang.

Place the car in gear, set the parking brake, and block the wheels, to prevent the vehicle from rolling. Place the jack under a section of the Mustang that's strong. The rear part of the front frame rails, behind the front wheels and by the torque boxes ahead of the rear wheels, is the best bet. This is especially true if you're using a hydraulic lift. On 5-liter cars, the fuel and brake lines run along the floorpan on the passenger side, so although you can support the jack on the outer edge of the floorpans, you shouldn't place the jack too far in, or it could damage them and mangle the lines.

When you begin jacking up the vehicle, have a wide pad on the top of the jack and preferably some thick pieces of wood on top of the pad. This helps distribute the load evenly and prevents the jack from damaging the underside of your Mustang. The best way to elevate the car is to use two jacks and do either the front or rear on both sides, having a colleague jack one side while you do the other.

If you're going to be working underneath, especially if you're raising the back of the car first, make sure the front wheels are blocked, to prevent the car from rolling.

Once the front or rear is in the air, you can move the axle stands into position. At the front, a good, sturdy place to put them is on the outer area of the front K-member, where it meets with the lower control arms. The farther out on the K-member you can place them, the better. At the back, place the stands on the outer edge of the rear axle for optimum stability.

When the car is fully supported, try moving it, to see if it rocks. If it's firmly secured on the axle stands, it won't move. Now the real work can begin.

Like any car, the 5-liter Mustang has some spots underneath better suited for jacking than others. At the front, the best point is the frame rails, just aft of where they come down from the lower firewall. This is one of the strongest areas of an otherwise flimsy unibody. If the car already has subframe connectors installed, you can rest the jack on the frame rail, near where the connectors attach to it at the front.

At the back, position the jack under the rear torque boxes, just ahead of the lower control arms. If your Mustang has subframe connectors, you can place the jack pad on these (see the next photo). The rear torque boxes are also one of the strongest structural areas on these cars. You can place the jack on the outer edge of the floorpans but never place the jack too far underneath the floors, because they aren't as sturdy here, plus fuel and brake lines run along the bottom.

If you have access, use a hydraulic lift like this. If you're using a floor jack and axle stands, placing a block of wood between the jacking point and the jack itself spreads the load evenly. This jack pad is positioned on the rear of the subframe connector, which is more than strong enough to support the weight.

PROJECT 2 ★ *Changing the Engine Oil*

Time: 30 minutes

Tools: Wrench, filter wrench, flat-blade screwdriver, paper towels, oil pan bucket, gloves

Talent: ★

Applicable years: All

Parts: New filter, fresh motor oil (minimum 5 quarts)

Tab: $25

Tip: Have a big enough container or used oil drum to catch the old oil.

Performance Improvement: Increase your engine's longevity and reliability

Changing your oil at regular intervals is one of the simplest and best things you can do to prolong the life of your Mustang's engine and improve its performance. Also change your oil if you're performing significant repairs to the cooling system, such as removing the timing cover, because coolant can leak from the jacket passages into the oil pan and contaminate the oil. Factory literature states that you should replenish the oil every 3,000 miles or 5,000 kilometers, though if you don't drive the car often, replace it at least twice a year.

Before you begin, find out what kind of oil to use. From the factory, 302 HOs used 10W30 oil, though if you live in a climate with extremely cold temperatures, 5W30 is recommended in winter, because the thinner viscosity flows better. (The "W" in multiweight oil stands for winter and indicates that the oil meets viscosity ratings for use at 0 degrees Fahrenheit.) For warmer temperatures and modified engines, thicker weight oils should be used.

Some individuals who own 5-liters swear by synthetics. The benefits of synthetics (such as more efficient lubrication and better heat resistance) are notable, but before rushing to your nearest parts store, factor in the age and mileage

on your 5-liter. If the engine has a healthy number of miles, along with older seals, and has used mineral-based oil since the beginning, stick with it. Synthetic oils do clean deposits and other sludge inside the engine, but they can clean it out so much that a once dry motor starts leaking everywhere. If the engine is a new crate motor or freshly rebuilt, with new seals, then for maximum effectiveness go for a synthetic brand

With the Mustang in the air and an oil drum or large container placed beneath the oil pan, begin removing the plugs. Start with the bottom one first, because it will allow most of the oil to drain out first and will make things less messy.

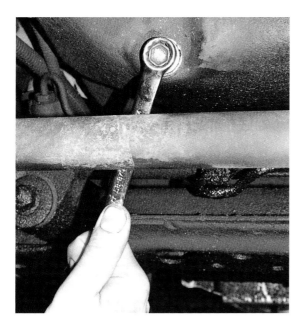

after the initial running in. (Break in the motor on mineral oil, because synthetics create so little friction that the rings may not seat properly.)

To perform an oil change, you need a funnel or drainage pan to catch the old oil and a used jug or oil can to collect and dispose of it. You'll also need a wrench, a replacement filter, and some old rags or paper towels. Wearing a pair of gloves is also a good idea, to prevent hot, dirty oil from getting on your hands.

Before changing the oil, start the car up and drive it around until the motor reaches operating temperature (this makes the old oil and any deposits drain out a lot more quickly). Pull the car back into the service area and raise it. The 302 V-8s in these Mustangs have a double-hump oil pan and two drain plugs, one at the front and one at the bottom. Taking note of the size of the plugs, move your funnel and canister into position below the bottom plug. Use a wrench to carefully loosen the plug, and the oil will begin to drain out.

Once it has, wipe the plug clean before reinstalling, and tighten it so no more oil dribbles. Then wipe the surrounding surface of the oil pan to remove any excess oil. Repeat the procedure with the front plug.

Once most of the oil has dribbled out of the bottom, retighten the bottom pan plug and remove the front one to drain the rest. After it has trickled out from the front plug too, retighten it and wipe the pan area surrounding it with a rag. Otherwise, oil deposits left behind from the old oil pouring out will drip.

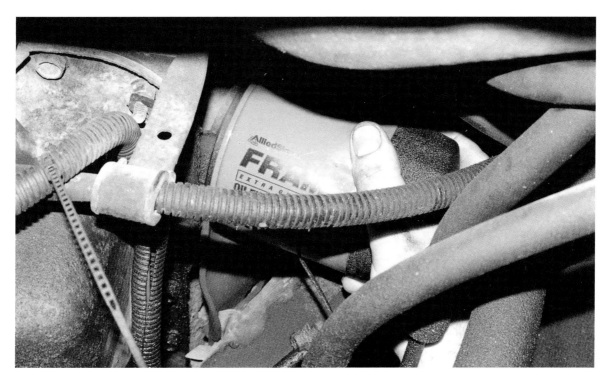

It's only really necessary to hand tighten oil filters, so your old one should come off with ease. If it doesn't, punch a screwdriver through it, which should give you enough leverage to help loosen it. Keep the oil can or drainage container below the filter, because the filter will still be full of oil, even if the sump has been drained.

When replacing your oil, do your homework before selecting a type and brand. On fairly stock 5-liters with a decent number of miles, a good-quality mineral oil, such as Castrol 10W40, will provide more than adequate lubrication and heat resistance. Only if you have a freshly built engine should you go with synthetics, and then only after break-in with mineral oil.

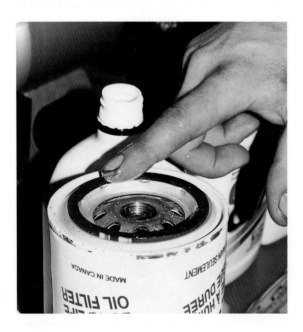

Before installing your new replacement filter, coat the gasket at the top with fresh engine oil all the way around, to provide a tight seal.

Next, remove the filter. Select the right replacement— Ford Motorcraft filters are a good and popular choice. To remove the filter, move a drain pan underneath it, place a rag over it, and twist the filter loose by hand. If it requires more effort, use a filter wrench or poke a screwdriver through it.

Before installing the new filter, use your finger to coat the gasket ring around the top with fresh engine oil. Install the filter and twist it until you feel resistance from the filter seat. Then tighten it another three-quarters turn by hand.

Lower the car to ground level and locate the oil filler cap on the right valve cover. Unscrew the cap and use a funnel to pour in the fresh oil. Pour four quarts in, then let it settle for a few minutes before checking the dipstick. If the oil is in the safe range on the dipstick, replace the filler cap. Start the engine, run it for about 60 seconds to get oil into the filter, and monitor the oil pressure gauge on the dash. It should read normal. Also look under the car, to check for any leaks around the pan plugs or filter while the engine is running.

Turn the motor off and add more oil until it reaches the full mark on the dipstick. On your first few trips afterward, check the oil level frequently and look for leaks.

PROJECT 3 ★ Removing the Air Silencer and Installing a High-Flow Air Filter

Time: 2 hours

Tools: Screwdriver, wrench, adjustable torque wrench

Talent: ★

Applicable years: 1979–1995 (filter); 1986–1995 (silencer)

Parts: Replacement air filter

Tab: $50

Performance Improvement: Improved power, throttle response, and drivability, decreased fuel consumption

Complementary Project: Timing advance

You can get extra power and performance from your 5-liter Mustang with a few tweaks. One of the easiest is to remove the factory air silencer and replace the stock air filter with a reusable high-flow one.

The early cars (1979 and 1982–1985) benefit considerably from a high-flow filter. From 1982 onward, these cars featured a massive dual-snorkel air cleaner assembly that housed a large-diameter but fairly shallow paper filter. At speed, the air pressurized upon entering the snorkel housing, but performance was weak during early acceleration. You can improve performance from a stop by ditching the stock paper filter for a less restrictive replacement, such as those available from K&N.

When Ford switched to sequential fuel injection (SEFI) for 1986, it created a more restrictive air path to the engine in an effort to silence air induction to the new intake assembly. Thus, when these 5-liters were rolling along the River Rouge assembly line, Ford fitted an air box that housed a flat-panel filter. It was hooked up to an inlet pipe on the right side that was in turn connected to the intake throttle body. An air silencer was also bolted to the right inner fender, behind the air box. Its sole purpose was to reduce noise as the air passed up into the air box. It also hampered airflow and hence performance. By removing this piece of plastic and ditching the stock panel filter for a less restrictive one, fuel-injected 5-liter owners can pick up an extra 5 horsepower.

To remove the silencer on these cars, you need decent clearance in the right front fender area, so jacking up the car and supporting it on axle stands at the front is a good idea. You'll also need to open the hood and remove the

lower stock air box assembly (the rectangular section that attaches to the cylindrical ducting). It's secured by three bolts at the top and bottom, along with a circle clip that secures it to the upper part of the assembly.

The air silencer will now be visible through an oval-shaped hole behind where the air box normally sits. To remove it, unscrew the three bolts that attach it to the fender (two at the top, one at the bottom). Then move underneath, to the wheelwell, and slowly pull out the

Installing a high-flow filter is usually one of the first things to do when you buy a 5-liter Mustang. These flow much better than the restrictive stock paper filters. K&N *(shown)* has long been the brand of choice, though other companies such as AFE, Green Filter, FRAM, and Holley also offer them.

Changing the filter on sequential fuel-injected Mustangs is a simple case of unfastening the clips that hold the filter housing together, pulling out the old stock filter, and installing the free-flowing replacement. The flat-panel housing and filter like this are found on 1986–1993 models. The 1994–1995 cars use a more efficient circular housing and filter assembly.

silencer. Once you've removed the silencer, put it in storage for safekeeping.

The next part is putting back the air box assembly and installing a replacement panel filter inside it. The K&N FilterCharger has long been the preferred direct-replacement panel filter for these cars, though other companies, such as Advance Flow Engineering, FRAM, and Holley, now offer filters tailored to 1986–1993 SEFI 5-liter Mustangs. The K&N FilterCharger and AFE Magnum Flow have fewer elements than the stock filter and are designed to improve airflow and pressurize air when the Mustang is at speed. They're also oil coated and thus washable and reusable (up to 25 times, or 10 years in the case of the K&N).

To remove the stock paper filter and replace it, undo the clips that hold the two pieces of the lower air box assembly together, pull out the old filter, and slide in the replacement. Some owners may want to ditch the stock air box completely, in favor of a conical filter, such as K&N's FIPK (FilterCharger Injection Performance Kit) or a cold air kit such as those from Moroso or BBK.

Although a conical filter is less restrictive than a panel one, it's also exposed to the rest of the engine bay and, thus, heat. Because it relies too much on air already inside the engine bay, it isn't as effective at collecting

cooler air as a sealed panel filter, despite its greater surface area and potential flow. The cold air kits have a kink in the tube housing and mount the filter through the right fender opening, where the air silencer normally sits. They're slightly better than conical filters, but their ability to boost horsepower depends largely on weather and air temperature outside. Even compared to a high-flow panel filter sealed inside the stock air box, their benefits are minimal.

If you own a 1994–1995 Mustang 5-liter, you're already ahead of the game—Ford installed a less restrictive silencer on these cars (it's still in the same location) and also a factory conical filter inside a plastic housing. These filters are similar to the FilterCharger and cold air kits available for Fox cars, but they have the advantage of being encased in a plastic housing. Installing a K&N or similar high-flow filter will therefore pay big dividends.

Some owners like to run their cars on a chassis dyno before and after performing this upgrade, so they can see the difference in horsepower and torque this project can make.

Besides the filter, take out your air silencer to add a couple of extra horsepower. Three bolts secure it to the right inner fender. Newer, 1994–1995 Mustangs have a less restrictive, small rubber tube that attaches to the cylindrical filter housing, which you can easily yank off *(seen here)*. Keep your silencer in a safe place once you take it off. They will become as sought after in the future as original Thermactor smog pumps are on classic Mach 1 and GT Mustangs today.

PROJECT 4 ★ *Performing a Tune-Up/Ignition Upgrade*

Time: 4 hours

Tools: Screwdriver, adjustable torque wrench, sockets

Talent: ★★★

Applicable years: 1982–1995

Parts: Replacement ignition wires, distributor cap, rotor, spark plugs, coil

Tab: $300

Performance Improvement: Improved power, drivability, and fuel consumption

Complementary Project: Timing advance

Given that they were conceived in the early post-energy-crisis marketplace, the factory Duraspark (carbureted) and Thick Film Ignition systems on 5-liter Mustangs aren't really that bad. They were designed to maximize fuel economy and reduce emissions and, like everything else, had to achieve their objectives at a cost deemed sensible by corporate bean counters.

While the factory setups, particularly Duraspark II and III and TFI, featuring its wide distributor cap and E-coil, are fairly good at what they do, extended use and attack from underhood heat ultimately take their toll. The coil can't generate the voltage it once did, and heat will eventually damage the plug wires, increasing their resistance and thus the chance of ignition crossfire or electromagnetic interference. One thing worth noting is that the factory replacement and upgraded Motorcraft spark plugs and distributor cap are pretty decent, and most 5.0 owners find that replacements from other manufacturers don't necessarily work any better.

If it's been awhile since the Mustang has had fresh plugs, along with a cap and rotor, replace them along with the rest of the ignition system. (Frequent plug changes are essential to keep your 5-liter running in top form, despite what some plug manufacturers may claim.) If your car is running with power adders and advanced timing, run a cooler plug than factory stock—the more power, the colder the plug. Cooler plugs are better for slower–burning, higher-octane fuel and their short

In its day, the factory ignition setup on 5-liter Mustangs, as on this SEFI engine, wasn't bad at all. But time and usage means that most cars could do with improved ignition hardware, especially if you plan on making more power than stock.

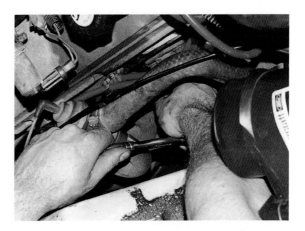

When upgrading/replacing ignition pieces, a new distributor cap and rotor should be on your list. The existing ones will often be worn and corroded, which can lead to increased electromagnetic interference and hence reduced performance and engine operating efficiency.

Use an adjustable torque wrench to remove the spark plugs as the greater leverage will probably make it easier to remove them. Be careful when accessing plug number 4, because it's partly hidden by the EGR tubing for the emissions gear.

Because the 5-liter Mustang is a darling of the aftermarket, many companies offer ignition components for it. These 8 mm replacement wires by Taylor Performance Products are a popular choice for street-going Mustangs and fit right in place of the stockers. Ford Racing Performance Parts (Motorsport), Accel, and Jacobs also offer quality wire sets for 5-liter applications.

Choosing the right plug depends largely on what your goals are for the car. Generally speaking, you'll want to use colder plugs for high-performance engines. These are so named because they have shorter insulator noses, to expel heat. Note the difference in length between the "cold" plug *(top)* and a factory stock one *(bottom)*.

insulator nose enables them to dissipate heat more effectively and help ward off detonation.

As far as other replacement ignition parts go, MSD, Accel, Jacobs, Mallory, Taylor, and Ford Racing Performance Parts (FRPP) all offer good-quality items for 5-liter applications. On most street 5.0s, a set of aftermarket 8 or 8.5 mm wires and replacement TFI coil, in conjunction with the stock replacement plugs, cap, and rotor, work well.

When replacing/upgrading the ignition system, the plugs and wires are usually the best place to start. Some aftermarket ignition wire sets are numbered, but for

others, you'll need to match up your replacement wires to the originals, to make sure the lengths correspond.

To avoid unnecessary aggravation, tackle one cylinder at a time. Start at the front, on the driver's side, and work front to rear; then do the same on the passenger side. (The 302's emissions pipe routing makes for limited access to cylinder number 4, at the back on the passenger side.) Remove each spark plug with a torque wrench and check its condition.

Reading plugs is a black art in many respects, but the color and condition will give you a basic idea of your

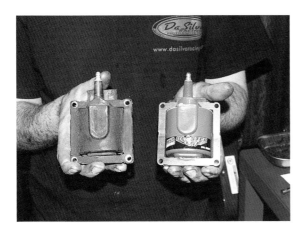

Part of your ignition upgrade should include a replacement coil. The one shown here is a direct bolt-in for the stocker *(left)* and provides a notable increase in voltage without any need for specialist mounting hardware.

Performing a fuel system flush when replacing the ignition will help your 5-liter's engine make the most of the improvements. Snap-on's Fuel System Cleaner uses compressed air to clean your Mustang's fuel system. It may be a bit more costly and complex than pouring fuel treatment cleaner in the gas tank every three months, but it's considerably more effective.

engine's overall health. Each plug, when removed, should have a reddish-brown tinge and slight electrode wear. If the plug is overtly black, the motor is running too rich; if you discover significant white deposits, it's running dangerously lean. If everything appears fine, gap the new plug. It should be in the 0.45-inch range on a normally aspirated engine and approximately 0.29–0.35 inch on cars running forced induction.

It's a good idea to coat the top threads with an anti-seize compound before installation. Then connect the bottom end of the replacement ignition wire to it and, using the original distributor cap as a guide, place the other end on the correct terminal of its replacement. Repeat the procedure for the other cylinders, until you've matched each wire correctly. Then remove the old cap and replace the rotor arm before installing the new cap over the distributor.

Some owners keep the plastic wiring-loom tab separators for appearance and safety—if so, note where each one goes before taking the ignition system apart. If your Mustang still has the original cap's dust cover, you may want to install it too, although it does generate quite a bit of heat. A lot of owners either leave it off or put it on only for shows.

Next on the list is coil replacement. On fuel-injected 5-liters, the TFI coils are more efficient and provide greater voltage to the plugs than the canister coils on earlier cars. Therefore, even if you have a carbureted 5.0, it's still worth switching to a TFI coil. MSD's Blaster TFI is a direct replacement for the factory E-coil and is great for street cars, because it slots right in place of the OEM piece. Other E-coils are similar in design, but some mount on their own brackets and require a drill and screwdrivers.

If your 5-liter has received more serious engine mods, especially those designed to make the engine rev beyond its stock max 4,000–5,000 rpm power band, consider an aftermarket ignition box. These capacitive discharge systems take the load off the TFI coil at higher rev ranges, where the coil finds it more difficult to recharge in the shorter time allowed to transform the voltage. By storing amplified battery voltage in a capacitor before sending it to the coil, these boxes enable the coil to fire more voltage to the plugs in a shorter period.

Fuel System Flush

When performing an ignition upgrade, it's wise to pay attention to the fuel system, especially if it's been a while since the Mustang received a full tune-up. An effective way to keep your SEFI 302 running in top form is to flush the fuel system every 18,000 miles, using a special fuel-system cleaner kit, such as the one from Snap-on. It includes special coupling lines that attach to the stock injector rails and link up to a canister that houses a mixture of system cleaner and fuel. It forces the mixture into the fuel system via air pressure once the motor is started and is one of the more effective ways of cleaning out sludgy deposits.

To do this, you'll need a special fuel-line lock-coupler tool kit, to remove part of the stock fuel rails and attach the pipes that come with the cleaner kit. Next, block the return fuel line by disconnecting the fuel pump, by the gas tank at the rear of the car. Then make sure the system is securely hooked up and start your 5.0's engine. Let it idle until all the liquid in the canister has been pumped through the fuel system and the engine starts to sputter. As a rule, the process takes about 20 minutes. The cleaner your engine, the less time it will take for the motor to stall.

Once the process is complete, switch off the engine and disconnect the system cleaner hardware before reinstalling your fuel rails and hooking up the fuel pump.

PROJECT 5 ★ *Advancing the Ignition Timing*

Time: 1 hour

Tools: Adjustable timing light, distributor wrench

Talent: ★★★

Applicable years: 1986–1995

Parts: None

Tab: $0

Tip: Run 12–14 degrees initial timing for best results.

Performance Improvement: Improved power and throttle response, decreased fuel consumption

Complementary Project: Ignition upgrade

An old hot-rod trick that works particularly well on 5-liter Mustangs is a timing advance. To do this, you'll need a distributor wrench and a good, multi-adjustable timing gun, like this one.

Another virtually free horsepower tip on 5-liter Mustangs is to advance the ignition timing. The sooner the engine can initiate the spark, the more time the spark has to work with the air/fuel mixture, allowing more complete combustion and increased power output. From the factory, and primarily to cut costs and optimize emissions, 5-liters came with fairly modest timing curves—anything from 6 to 10 degrees before top dead center (BTDC).

As enthusiasts began to learn about the fuelie 302 and its hardware, they discovered that advancing ignition timing to 14 degrees initial paid big dividends. One writer/owner, Neil Van Oppre, made 5-liter history. By including the timing advance as an integral part of his 10-minute tune-up, he saw his 1987 LX hatchback go from running 14-second to 12-second ETs at the drags.

Many 5-liters on the road will already have the timing advanced, but some totally stock cars are still out there, so it's worth finding out just how much timing you're running. Advancing the timing will boost fuel mileage as well as performance, though it will increase emissions from your 5.0's dual tailpipes.

Before carrying out this project, you'll need a timing light and a distributor wrench. The key is to advance the distributor and run as much timing as possible, short of detonation. Detonation is uncontrolled—rather than controlled, progressive—burning of the air/fuel mixture in the combustion chamber. Detonation causes flame fronts in the combustion chambers that hit each other,

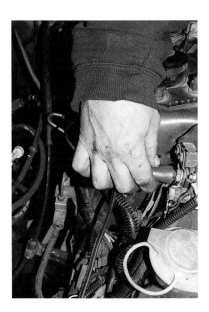

Once you've marked the crank damper with your intended setting, hook up the timing gear to your ignition. Start by connecting the plug to the starter solenoid by the left inner fender.

Attach the clip at the other end to the plug wire of your choice, so the light can flash when the spark is fired to that plug. Now you're ready to pull out the SPOUT connector and begin.

With your SPOUT connector unfastened or the vacuum line blocked, use the timing gun and a distributor wrench to adjust ignition timing to the correct setting. Most normally aspirated 5.0s like to run between 10 and 14 degrees initial timing BTDC. It's also worth doing this if you've just bought the Mustang, to find out how much initial timing the car is already running.

resulting in a surge in cylinder combustion pressure. A related condition, preignition, occurs when the air/fuel charge ignites from excess heat and pressure before the spark plug fires.

Detonation and preignition create pressure and temperature extremes in the engine and resist proper piston movement. Combined with high compression or forced induction, the potential is serious engine damage, including blown head gaskets, damaged pistons, and bent rods. Either way, fixing this problem is expensive, so you'll want to avoid it at all costs.

Before advancing the timing, clean off the crankshaft damper and mark it with the setting you want. (As a general rule, you probably won't want to run more than 14 degrees initial on a regularly street-driven car, though some stick-shift 5.0s will run more—up to around 18 degrees is not unheard of). Then, on fuel-injected cars, disconnect the EFI SPOUT connector (located by the distributor from 1986–1993 or by the air box assembly on 1994 and 1995). On carbureted cars, block the vacuum line to the distributor.

Using the timing light and distributor wrench, slowly advance the setting by single-degree intervals until you hear a ping or knock (this means you've arrived at detonation). When you hear this, retard the timing until the knock disappears. (You can also use an external knock sensor, which sounds an alarm when the engine reaches detonation.) Now you have optimal initial timing. Reconnect the SPOUT connector or vacuum line, and you're done!

If your car is running with optimal timing, you'll also want to run a higher octane fuel (91–94 is recommended for street cars). The higher the octane, the more slowly the fuel burns, and the greater its resistance to detonation. To maximize results, it's a good idea to incorporate a timing advance with a basic ignition upgrade (Project 4), because the factory system was designed to work only with stock parameters and doesn't get better with age.

PROJECT 6 ★ *Installing Underdrive Pulleys*

Time: 3 hours

Tools: Screwdriver, adjustable torque wrench, sockets

Talent: ★★★

Applicable years: 1979–1995

Parts: Underdrive pulley kit, replacement belt

Tab: $200

Tip: Use a Cobra water pump pulley on your Fox 5-liter.

Performance Improvement: Improved power

Complementary Project: Cooling system upgrade, timing advance

Available from March Performance and ASP, underdrive pulleys reduce parasitic loss of power and torque by slowing down the turning speed of the accessory drive. They often come in two- or three-piece sets—crank and water pump or alternator, crank, and water pump. If you tend to drive your Mustang on the street, be careful, because the slower turning speed of the underdrive pulleys can affect cooling (1979–1993 cars) and can reduce voltage output from the alternator, resulting in a poor charge at idle speed.

The best solution for a regularly street-driven Mustang is to use the large underdrive crank pulley and a 1993 Cobra water pump pulley (for 1979–1993 cars, available from Ford Racing Performance Parts). The Cobra pulley is of smaller diameter than the aftermarket underdrive water pump pulley, which means it rotates more quickly. Therefore, you gain a power increase without having to compromise the effectiveness of your stock cooling system.

Unplug the negative battery cable before turning your attention to the factory radiator shroud. Before you begin unfastening it, check the condition of your factory clutch fan (if it's still in place). The 1979 5-liters use a flex-blade fan, and 1982–1993 models use a rigid plastic clutch type fan. (The1994–1995 cars use a far more efficient electric fan, so you don't have to worry about fan removal to access the water pump and crank pulley.)

The rigid plastic clutch fan is prone to cracking where the blades meet the hub, and over time the clutch mechanism can start to slip. Try to move the fan forward and backward, to see if the blades wobble. If so, you'll need to replace the fan and clutch assembly. Also try spinning the

fan with the car at rest. If it doesn't turn at all, or freewheels, again the clutch assembly is worn and will need replacing.

Unbolt the fan and clutch assembly by undoing the bolts that secure it to the water pump pulley. Then unbolt the shroud (it attaches to the radiator at the header panel with two bolts) and lift the shroud and fan out of the engine compartment. If your clutch is worn but the fan is okay, you can remove the former by undoing the bolts that attach it to the plastic fan. When replacing the clutch, it's a good idea to upgrade to the Special Service Package/OPEC-style clutch with revised release points,

All 5-liter Mustangs use a single serpentine belt drive for the accessories—so named because it snakes between the drive pulleys (shown is a 1992 Mustang GT with the stock clutch fan driven off the water pump). Driving the accessories robs the engine of quite a bit of power, so installing underdrive pulleys is a popular and effective performance modification.

Probably the best-known aftermarket supplier of replacement pulleys for domestic performance vehicles is March Performance, which offers both two- and three-piece underdrive pulley sets for 5-liter Mustangs.

With the stock crank pulley off, bolt the replacement on the end of the crank balancer, using the stock holes for the bolts, as seen here.

which will improve power and cooling. Performance Parts, Inc. (703-742-6207) is a good source for these.

Next, remove the drivebelt. All 5-liter Mustangs use a single serpentine belt of a V-ribbed design to drive the accessories. The accessory drive incorporates self-adjusting automatic belt tensioners and a wear indicator. If the belt has been on the Mustang awhile, check the indicator and also look at the belt's overall condition. If it's fraying or cracked, replace it—installing underdrive pulleys often puts a strain on the cooling system, because the fan will be turning more slowly, and a worn belt exaggerates the problem.

It's worth checking the belt routing. If your Mustang hasn't been repainted under the hood, chances are the emissions and belt routing stickers will still be in place. Two types of belt routing are employed on 5-liter Mustangs—one with air conditioning, one without. Note which yours has before removing and replacing the belt,

For most street cars, consider going with two-piece pulleys like these, which have a replacement crank pulley (the larger one) and water pump pulley (the smaller one). Three-piece sets add an alternator pulley, but the slower turning speed can cause voltage problems and hard starting.

This 302 engine already has the two-piece crank and water pump pulleys installed and is shown removed from the car for illustration. Above the water pump pulley is the factory tensioner for the serpentine belt system.

so you can route it correctly (this may seem obvious, but you'd be surprised how easy it is to overlook).

If you own a 1979–1984 5-liter Mustang, pull the tensioner away from the belt and hold it to remove the belt. On 1985 and later Mustangs, use a breaker bar and socket to rotate the tensioner and slip the belt off. Then you can unbolt your crank and water pump (and alternator if you're doing three-piece) pulleys and install the new ones.

With the pulleys on, grab your new belt and make sure it's free from dirt and debris. Make sure the tensioner is held back while you install the belt. Once it's on, release the tensioner, and you're all set. Now you can reinstall your clutch fan and radiator shroud.

PROJECT 7 ★ *Installing Aftermarket Headers*

Time: 5 hours

Tools: Adjustable torque wrench, sockets, WD-40, gloves, Sharpie marker, scraper, fine sander, copper sealant

Talent: ★★★★

Applicable years: 1985–1995

Parts: New headers, flange bolts, gaskets

Tab: $400

Tip: Ceramic coat your headers inside and out for better performance and longer life.

Performance Improvement: Improved scavenging, horsepower, torque, and throttle response

Complementary Project: High-flow H- or X-pipe and cat-back exhaust

An engine is nothing but a glorified air pump. If you force a greater amount of air in to increase power, you also need to expel the byproduct as efficiently as possible. On many performance cars, the stock exhaust system is a major Achilles' heel that prevents the engine from realizing its greater potential. The 5-liter Mustang is no different, though considering the systems offered on many rival cars, the factory exhaust isn't too bad (especially from 1986 up).

Early Fox V-8 cars had heavy, restrictive, cast-iron manifolds mated to a restrictive Y-pipe and a single exhaust and muffler with twin outlets on the left side. For 1985, Ford installed nickel-coated tubular steel "shorty" headers, a bigger Y-pipe, and a 2 1/4–inch diameter stainless-steel cat-back exhaust with dual tips. The following year, they ditched the Y-pipe for a four-cat H-pipe, giving the 5-liter Mustang a true dual exhaust for the first time.

The shorty headers, thanks in part to their separate tubes (versus a common one for all four exhaust ports on each side, like the old manifolds), worked extremely well for factory parts and were instrumental in providing the 302 with so much torque. However, they still impose restrictions on exhaust gas flow and scavenging (the sucking of the depleted charge out of the combustion chamber by a negative pressure wave that comes back through the exhaust system to the engine). These restrictions become more noticeable once you start playing with your motor. For that reason, many owners choose to upgrade to a set of aftermarket headers.

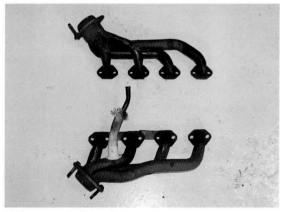

A great way to help your 5-liter make more power is to install replacement exhaust headers. The stock pieces that came on these cars from 1985–1995 are remarkably good for a mass-production vehicle. However, they incorporate a number of kinks, to provide clearance for sockets when installing them, which hamper exhaust flow. At the top is a 1986–1993 factory header; the bottom shows the 1994–1995 pieces (note the location of the EGR tube on the newer headers).

On most 5-liter Mustangs, you'll probably need to spray some WD-40 on the header bolts before you can remove them. Once you've taken out the bolts (and make sure you account for all of them), you should be able to loosen and simply pull the factory header off the cylinder head and carefully ease it out of the engine bay.

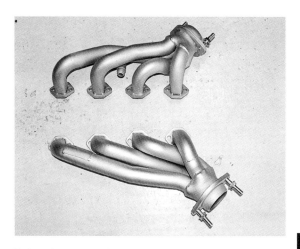

Today, a huge range of aftermarket headers is available for 5-liter Mustangs. Among the most popular for regular street-driven cars are the MAC 1 5/8-inch-diameter shorties, which have gained a deserved reputation for exceptional quality and excellent fit. They're also designed to work with the stock emissions gear, making them a bolt-on-and-forget-it deal.

Part of the problem with the stockers is that they incorporate a number of indentations, to provide clearance and ease of installation on the assembly line, and these crimps hamper exhaust flow. By bolting on a set of less restrictive headers, your 302 can gain a noticeable increase in horsepower and torque, especially when combined with other exhaust and engine tweaks.

Replacement headers for a 5-liter involve several important considerations. Should you go with unequal-length shorties, equal-length, or long-tube headers? For 1979–1995 5.0s, the aftermarket offers a large number of replacements (BBK and MAC are popular), but some of them work better than others for specific applications. (Note that if you have a 1985 5-liter, you'll need a heat valve for your driver's-side header).

When selecting headers for your Mustang, diameter as well as style should also influence choice—most headers designed for 5.0s are available in 1 1/2-, 1 5/8-, and 1 3/4-inch sizes. On most street-going 5.0s, consider a set of 1 1/2- or 1 5/8-diameter unequal-length shorties. They're designed as a direct bolt-on replacement for the factory pieces and mate with the factory H- or Y-pipe assemblies, and they have plumbing provisions in the same location as the stockers for the oxygen sensors and emissions hardware (essential if you're driving your 5-liter on the street).

Although shorties may yield less horsepower increase when compared with longer and larger-diameter headers, they're more effective torque producers. The larger the pipe diameter, the greater the flow and the lower the velocity, which causes torque to suffer at the expense of high-end horsepower. Thus, on a stock 302 that makes its maximum grunt typically between 3,000 and 5,000 rpm, a massive big-bore exhaust with 1 3/4- or 2-inch-diameter long tubes, for all its flow capability, isn't going to do much.

Equal-length and long-tube headers are best reserved for street/strip and race applications, because they're more effective on engines making greater horsepower at and above the stock rpm operating range. There, the motor can really benefit from their increased scavenging. Also, because they're more strip oriented, you're often walking the line when it comes to emissions. Many don't have emissions provisions, and on those that do, the extra length of the headers relocates the oxygen sensors too far from the engine's exhaust ports, preventing the sensors from warming up and hence working properly to reduce tailpipe pollution.

Installing equal-length and long-tube systems also requires a bit more ingenuity if you want to run a stock-style exhaust, because you'll require a shorter (and sometimes custom) H-pipe assembly in conjunction with a cat-back for a full-length exhaust. Custom-sized long tubes are often used on a full-out race car, on which you'd probably run open headers anyway. Therefore, emissions compliance, length, and H-pipe compatibility would typically not be an issue. Since this project concerns a street car, we'll stick with shorty replacements.

Start the project with a cold motor. It's also a good idea to wear protective gloves. For the removal and installation, put the car on a lift or jack stands and

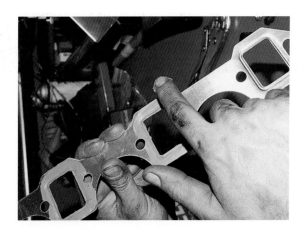

MAC also supplies quality replacement copper gaskets with its shorty headers. Coat the new gaskets with copper sealant to prevent any exhaust leaks. As many enthusiasts will tell you, not only do leaks compromise flow and scavenging (and thus horsepower and torque), they'll also drive you nuts once you get behind the wheel.

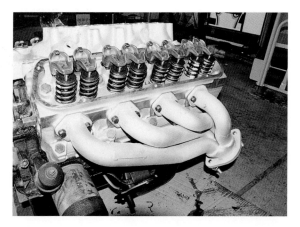

Along with gaskets, MAC supplies brand-new header bolts for a tight, OEM-style fit and even a special long bolt for the factory dipstick tube. A good idea before installing the headers is to get them ceramic coated inside and out. This will improve heat dissipation and exhaust scavenging and will reduce the chance of discoloration and corrosion.

remove the H- or Y-pipe assembly (it's secured by flange studs). Then lower the car a little (if on the lift) so you can reach under the hood and locate the header bolts, where the flanges attach to the cylinder heads. (The stock headers have individual flanges, whereas many replacements do not.) If you own a 1985 Mustang, remove the heat valve on your driver's-side header; if you own a 1994–1995, locate and remove the exhaust gas recirculation (EGR) tube that connects to the passenger-side header.

Then, using a torque wrench, remove the flange bolts from one header at a time, making sure you don't misplace any of them. On stock 302s, you'll find a hoist hook bolted to the factory headers, at the front on the driver's side and the rear on the passenger side. Ford installed these to facilitate hoisting the engine out of the car; however, they won't work with aftermarket headers.

Another good idea just before removing the bolts is to pop the ignition wires and remove the plugs. Not only does it make life easier (just make sure you mark each wire), it prevents you from damaging the plugs when fiddling around with the headers.

If your header bolts are rusted and seized, spray some WD-40 on them and let it penetrate for a few hours before attempting to remove them. It's worth taking your time removing the bolts and oil dipstick tube. Once you've done this, carefully pull each header out, either from the top or through the bottom, depending on how much clearance you have.

Next are the header gaskets. If the gasket is old, it may not come off easily, but you need to scrape away all the

material. If you don't, your headers will leak, even with new gaskets. After scraping, use a sander to smooth the surface down (be especially careful if your Mustang has aluminum heads). Aftermarket unequal-length shorties are usually designed as bolt-ons, so they'll match the exhaust ports on the heads and the flanges on the factory or direct-replacement H- or Y-pipe.

A good idea before installing the replacement headers is to get them ceramic coated, inside and out. This will help ward off discoloration and corrosion and will dissipate exhaust heat more effectively, helping power and torque.

Many replacement headers, such as the BBK and MAC shorties, come with replacement header bolts (including a special one for the long dipstick tube), along with a set of gaskets. When installing the new items, remember to swap over the heat valve on your 1985 or the EGR tube on the passenger-side header from your 1994–1995 car. Also coat the area around the exhaust ports and header gaskets with copper sealant or a similar product.

Most aftermarket headers are designed as direct replacements, so installation is basically the reverse of removing the factory pieces. Make sure you torque the bolts to the correct specs. Fit new collector gaskets and reinstall the H-pipe. Once you're done, start the engine to check for any leaks.

If all is well, your replacement headers should provide a notable improvement in both performance and sound, but for best results, combine this project with upgrading the rest of the exhaust.

PROJECT 8 ★ *Installing a High-Flow H-Pipe*

Time: 2 hours

Tools: Adjustable torque wrench, sockets, oxygen sensor socket, WD-40, gloves

Talent: ★★

Applicable years: 1986–1995

Parts: New H-pipe, flange bolts, gaskets

Tab: $380

Tip: Choose a pipe with high-flow cats for best results on your street Mustang.

Performance Improvement: Improved exhaust flow, horsepower, torque, throttle response

Complementary Project: New exhaust headers and a cat-back exhaust

ENGINE

On 5-liter Mustangs, the factory exhaust consists of three distinct elements—the manifolds (1979 and 1982–1984) or headers (1985–1995), Y- or H-pipe, and mufflers and tailpipe assembly. If you're replacing your factory manifolds or headers, it would also be wise to upgrade the Y- or H-pipe assembly.

The 1979 and 1982–1985 5-liters had a restrictive Y-pipe that mated to the exhaust, though for 1985, the diameter of the Y-pipe increased from 2 to 2 1/4 inches, to correspond to the new headers and cat-back dual exhaust. For 1986, Ford stepped up to the plate and replaced it with a 2 1/4-inch-diameter H-pipe assembly (so named because it had a single pipe on each side that incorporated a crossover tube to increase torque and reduce exhaust noise while minimizing emissions). It incorporates two pre-catalytic converters right behind the collectors on each side and a further two cats just before the crossover pipe.

In its day, the factory H-pipe wasn't a bad setup and was partly responsible for making the 302 such a strong street engine, though it was designed to work with other stock exhaust components. If you install aftermarket headers and mufflers, the stock H-pipe will pose a major restriction. (Some 5-liters known as OPEC Mustangs—destined for the Middle East, where unleaded gasoline was not widely available—came from the factory with special non-cat export H-pipes, providing a little more horsepower, though these cars cannot be driven on North American soil in stock form, because they lack emission controls.)

If you've recently bought a 5-liter, find out what kind of Y- or H-pipe the car has. One thing to note is that 1986-and-up 5-liters required a new double-hump transmission crossmember to clear the H-pipe. If you have an earlier Fox Mustang and want to install a complete dual exhaust, you'll need to source one of these crossmembers—otherwise, you won't be able to install an H-pipe properly.

If you own a 1986–1988 5-liter and it still has the stock H-pipe system in place, the converters were recalled, so it's worth checking with a Ford service department to see if this has been performed. When I bought my 1986 GT a few years ago, it still had the original H-pipe. My

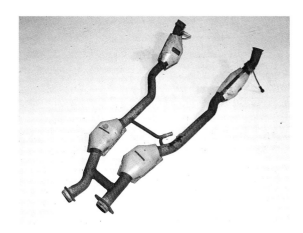

Here's the factory H-pipe found on 1986–1995 V-8 Mustangs. The tubing is of 2 1/4-inch-diameter and has two pre-cats ahead of the main converters (to warm up the oxygen sensors, minimizing emissions) and a crossover tube. Note the location of the twin oxygen sensors and the single pipe just forward of the main converters, which hooks up to the 5-liter's air injection system and smog pump.

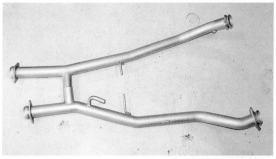

MAC is one of the most popular vendors for replacement H-pipes. The off-road H-pipe *(top)* and Pro-Chamber *(bottom)*, provide a welcome increase over the stock system but don't incorporate cats and are thus strictly for off-road racing. They also sacrifice usable torque when installed on most street 5-liters.

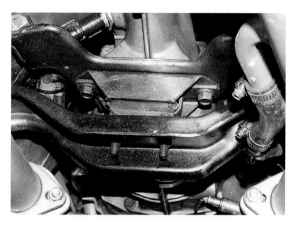

If you're installing an H-pipe on a 1985-or-earlier 5-liter that originally came with a single Y-pipe exhaust, you'll need to source a double-hump rear crossmember like this one, to provide clearance for the dual pipes.

When installing your replacement H-pipe, pay special attention to the front flanges, and make sure you have sufficient clearance to avoid damaging the oxygen sensors. Using a special socket helps.

local dealership fitted a free replacement, because the original converters were defective.

With 5-liters being so responsive to bolt-ons and the stock four-cat H-pipe posing a restriction, some owners in the early days removed the factory cats and bolted on a homemade or Ford Racing Performance Parts off-road H-pipe. Still others would hollow out the cats on their stock H-pipes. The latter isn't recommended, because it provides minimal performance gains while violating emissions laws.

If you want to retain stock appearance and performance and your cats are toast—either hollowed or blocked—you can still obtain H-pipe replacements from Ford (though supply is very limited) or a specialist vendor if you're lucky. For most 5-liter owners who crave greater-than-stock performance, the solution is to fit a larger-diameter H- or X-pipe replacement assembly.

These replacements come with cats or as "export" off-road assemblies. When considering removing and upgrading your stock H- or Y-pipe, it's best to work with a specialist Mustang or muffler shop, especially if you're new to 5.0 ownership. They can help you remove the stock assembly and will steer you toward a suitable replacement.

The stock H-pipe has four flange bolts where it mates with the headers and four more at the back, where it connects with the mufflers. When removing it, you'll need to disconnect the twin oxygen sensors and slide out the hangers that secure the H-pipe to the transmission mounts.

Sometimes the flange bolts are in good shape and can be reused on your replacement H-pipe. However, given that most 5-liters are over a decade old and will have covered a decent number of miles, the problem of seized

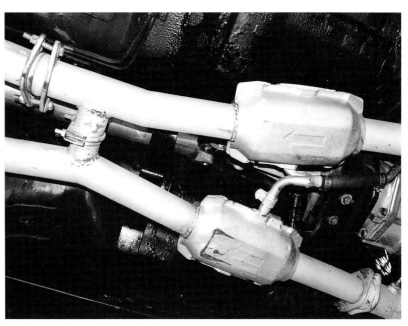

Here's an ideal setup for the street—a 2 1/2-inch MAC H-pipe with high-flow cats, as shown, completed and installed on a 1991 GT. Note how it incorporates the fitting to mate with the air injection system.

choice to free up extra horsepower, they tend to sacrifice torque and drivability for high-end horsepower. Therefore, they're best limited to off-road and more serious street/strip applications.

X-pipes are so named because they have exhaust tubes that cross over in an X configuration. This allows exhaust pulses to select the tailpipe that offers minimum resistance without the reversion that occurs with H-pipe assemblies because of their configuration. Although in theory this is more beneficial, using an X-pipe won't always produce the desired result, especially on a mild street 5.0. Also, many of them (even the ones with cats) make it tougher for your car to pass emissions than using an H-pipe, because of the location of the converters.

For most street-going 5-liter Mustangs, the best route is an H-pipe incorporating high-flow cats. Besides being less restrictive than the stock H-pipe, these high-flow pipes provide a welcome increase in torque for street cars yet still enable your 5-liter to pass emissions with flying colors.

Most of the high-flow converter H-pipes, such as those from BBK and MAC, dispense with the stock-style pre-cats and are available in 2 1/2-inch-diameter sizes. Besides being a bolt-in installation when combined with shorty headers and stock or replacement mufflers, they have emissions plumbing in the same location as the stock H-pipe and are therefore virtually an OEM fit. You can simply swap the oxygen sensors from the old H-pipe to the new (provided they're in good condition).

If you have a more serious motor, especially if you run forced induction, along with steeper rear-end gears, consider an X-pipe assembly from companies such as Dr. Gas, BBK, or Bassani. You'll really be able to benefit from the more efficient flow these systems provide for a high-horsepower engine. Dr. Gas offers only kits without cats, for racing, which have to be assembled and welded before installation. They're of exceptional quality, however, and are derived from experience on the NASCAR circuit. BBK and Bassani offer X-pipes with and without converters, giving 5.0 owners a bit more flexibility at the hi-po end of things.

bolts, studs, and corroded fittings will more than likely rear its ugly head. Therefore, a supply of WD-40 and an extra pair of experienced hands is particularly helpful.

Be careful when removing the H-pipe, because you can easily damage the oxygen sensors, which are expensive to replace. A special oxygen-sensor socket, if you can get one, fits into tighter confines than a traditional socket and will reduce the risk of sensor damage. This is particularly useful on the passenger side, where the location of the transmission mount hanger severely limits clearance.

Check the end color of each sensor. On a healthy engine, the tips should be gray. Black means carbon buildup, indicating that the engine is running rich. If so, the converters may be clogged, and the sensors will be no good (malfunctioning sensors will also contribute to rough engine running and sluggish acceleration).

Do your homework when selecting a replacement H-pipe. While many 5-liter Mustang owners in North America swap the factory setup for off-road non-cat H-pipes on their street-driven Mustangs, doing so, like hollowing out your stock cats, is illegal in most states and Canada and may expose you to a hefty fine. Although non-cat H-, Pro-Chamber, and (to an ever greater extent) X-pipe systems, such as those from Dr. Gas, may be less restrictive than the stocker and may seem a logical

PROJECT 9 ★ *Installing Replacement Mufflers*

Time: 5 hours

Tools: Adjustable torque wrench, sockets, socket wrench, WD-40, tubing cutter, gloves, access to a MIG welder

Talent: ★★★

Applicable years: 1985–1995 (1979–1984 may need modifications)

Parts: New mufflers, flow tubes, tailpipes, brackets, bolts, gaskets

Tab: $400

Tip: Choose a good-quality two- or three-chamber muffler for best results on your street car.

Performance Improvement: Improved exhaust flow, horsepower, torque, throttle response

Complementary Project: New exhaust headers and a high-flow H-pipe

Like the rest of the factory exhaust, the stock 2 1/4-inch-diameter mufflers and tailpipes on 1985–1993 Mustangs, good as they are, are still restrictive. Swapping them for a quality cat-back system will pay big dividends not only from a performance aspect but also from an acoustical one. (If you own an earlier 5.0 and are not too concerned about originality, ditching the restrictive single exhaust should be one of your priorities.) The 302 H.O. V-8 is one of the most distinctive-sounding engines around, and a good set of mufflers, besides freeing up horsepower and torque, will only enhance its wonderful rumble.

When choosing a set of mufflers and tailpipes, doing your homework is essential to getting the most performance and value for your hard-earned money—the range of mufflers and tailpipes available for 5-liters is truly staggering. Select a muffler and tailpipe size that at least corresponds in diameter to your H- or X-pipe assembly, to effectively expel hot exhaust gases. This becomes particularly important when you're forcing more air into the engine, because the huge volumes of exhaust generated won't have enough room to expand with stock-diameter exhaust and mufflers. Also, a smaller H-pipe combined with larger mufflers will hamper exhaust flow, even on a stock engine.

Another important consideration is interior noise. A big-bore, low-restriction cat-back may sound great at idle or outside the car on the street, but when you're cruising along the highway, the unending drone generated by some mufflers can be downright irritating. Ford corrected this resonance problem on the stock cat-back

system by making the left muffler longer than the right (and if you look closely at stock Mustangs, you'll notice this). Most aftermarket mufflers, by contrast, are of equal length, to reduce production costs, so if noise is a factor, pay attention to muffler design. (The baffled, multichambered Flowmasters are popular because they damp noise more effectively than some other systems, without sacrificing flow.)

Your particular 5-liter model is another influential factor in muffler and tailpipe choice. Most aftermarket mufflers are designed to work with 2 1/2-inch tailpipes. These come as part of a complete cat-back exhaust kit or

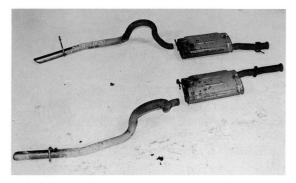

Stock cat-back dual exhaust systems on 5-liter Mustangs are among the least restrictive of factory installed pieces, but swapping them for a large-diameter aftermarket setup will still produce a noticeable improvement in power, torque, and exhaust tone. One muffler and flow tube on the stock system is slightly longer than the other, to improve resonance.

can be purchased or fabricated separately and bolted to the muffler flanges. If you choose the former, buy a muffler and tailpipes designed for your particular 5-liter. Most aftermarket systems designed for these cars that include tailpipes feature tips that clear the rear axle and shoot straight back to the bumper.

A 1987–1993 Mustang GT presents a few problems because of the rear valance, which required the OEM tailpipes to turn down at the tips for sufficient clearance. Some 1987–1993 GT Mustang owners buy systems designed for non-valanced 5-liters, then drill holes in the GT rear valance and send the pipes through—not a look all owners will like. An alternative is to install a 1993 Cobra valance, which provides cutouts for the tailpipes. Today, there are more choices. Flowmaster, MAC, Borla, and others offer full cat-back kits to fit both valanced GT and non-valanced 5-liter Mustangs. The systems these three companies offer are of exceptional quality and fit well.

While Flowmaster mufflers and tips (particularly the two- and three-chamber designs) continue to be popular because of their combination of flow, excellent fit, and interior noise reduction, the MAC, Borla, and Edelbrock 2 1/2-inch cat-back systems are also excellent choices. Da Silva Racing, a Mustang speed shop with years of experience installing Mustang exhausts, particularly recommends the MAC Flowpath cat-back for 5.0s, for its combination of fit, quality, ease of installation, and sound. The MAC system is easy to install, because it comes with most of the tailpipe section already joined to the back of the mufflers, whereas this is usually a separate piece on most aftermarket cat-backs.

Most replacement mufflers and tailpipes designed for 5-liters are a direct bolt-in, though as mentioned, if you buy the mufflers separately, make a note of the pipe diameter; for optimum results it should be at least the same as the H-pipe assembly.

For years, one of the most popular replacement mufflers has been the multichambered Flowmasters *(top)*. These pieces lend a delightful exhaust note that has become synonymous with modified 5-liter Mustangs. More recently, MAC *(bottom)* has jumped on the bandwagon with high-quality, high-flow replacement mufflers, including stainless-steel ones such as this.

Most complete cat-back exhaust kits come with fresh flanges and bolts, such as this Flowmaster system, shown installed on a 1992 Mustang. The bolts on the inside of the muffler/tailpipe secure it to the factory hangers on the frame. Use anti-seize compound on all the bolts and fittings, to help prevent them from rusting.

ENGINE

31

When installing exhaust components, start with the tailpipes. If you own a 1987–1993 Mustang GT, source tailpipes that turn down, to clear the rear valance. Note the perch that attaches to the rubber hanger, found on both stock and replacement tailpipes.

As on the other exhaust projects, removing and replacing the mufflers and tailpipes will go more smoothly if done in conjunction with a Mustang shop or someone with considerable experience. Start with a cold engine and soak the connections with WD-40 for several hours. To carry out this job, put the Mustang on jack stands or a lift, if possible.

Wearing gloves to protect your hands, first remove the H-pipe assembly. Then remove the tailpipes. They attach to the mufflers by flanges and secure to the chassis at the rear by a steel mounting bracket and rubber hanger on each side. Cut the muffler from the tailpipe right by the flange bolts at the front and pull off the muffler. Repeat the process for the other side.

Undo the rubber mounts and brackets that secure the tailpipes to the chassis. Carefully slide the tailpipe assembly backward until it's clear of the rear axle. Repeat the procedure for the other side. Finally, unbolt the flow tubes in front of each muffler and slide them off.

When installing the new aftermarket exhaust pieces, start with the tailpipes again, followed by the mufflers and the front flow tubes. Check the fit of each component before securing it. Also weld the seams (a MIG welder is recommended) between the mufflers, flow tubes, and tailpipes, to prevent leakage. Use fresh flange bolts, fittings, gaskets, rubber mounts, and brackets for added safety. Coat the flanges and bolts in lithium grease or some kind of anti-seize compound to help protect against corrosion.

Once you've installed your new cat-back, bolt up the H-pipe and make sure the oxygen sensors are hooked up properly. Start the car and take it for a test drive to make sure there are no leaks. The sound will definitely be worth the half day's work!

PROJECT 10 ★ *Choosing and Prepping Replacement Cylinder Heads*

Time: As long as it takes

Tools: Mustang specialty magazines and books, somebody with lots of experience modifying 5-liter Mustangs

Talent: ★★★★

Applicable years: All

Parts: New cylinder heads

Tab: $2,000–$2,500

Tip: Be careful when selecting heads, and bring a case of beer to the machine shop when porting or flow testing your heads.

Performance Improvement: Improved airflow, horsepower, torque, throttle response

Complementary Project: New intake assembly

Your engine's cylinder heads are crucial to its ability to produce power. When it comes to 5-liter Mustangs, the right heads can make or break your combination. All the exhaust and intake work in the world won't be any good unless you combine it with the right cylinder heads.

Given the popularity of the 5.0 today, choosing the right heads for your Mustang can be daunting, considering the many manufacturers and designs to choose from. From daily driver to weekend strip warrior, there's a set of heads to match. What you decide to use on your 5-liter depends on the requirements. Most owners drive their cars primarily on the street, so bang for the buck, drivability, and emissions are paramount.

For a factory stock engine, the OEM heads installed on the 5.0 really aren't bad and were improved over the years. In 1986, when Ford introduced sequential fuel injection on the 302 HO, they also raised the engine's compression ratio from 8.4:1 to 9.2:1 and cast new heads, coded E6SE, with shrouded, high-swirl combustion chambers. These were designed to improve emissions, but the downside was that their design severely restricted airflow and, combined with a relatively small intake tract, seriously choked the 1986 5.0, making it a poor top-end breather.

The following year, Ford rectified the situation by enlarging the intake tract and installing less restrictive heads—the E5TE and later E7TE. These were derived from a 1985 truck casting (the original tooling for the 85 HO heads had been scrapped) and featured 1.78- and 1.45-inch-diameter intake and exhaust valves, respectively. These bigger valves mandated a switch to lower-compression pistons with valve reliefs (the 1986 ones were flattops).

The resulting change was a noticeable increase in both power and acceleration. In fact, during the early days of 5-liter tuning, porting these stock heads could generate surprisingly impressive horsepower and torque numbers for relatively little cash. However, that was then. Advances in technology and the affordability of

One of the most popular notions in the 5-liter Mustang world is that bolting on a set of replacement cylinder heads will provide the most significant increase in power, torque, and performance, because the stock heads are so restrictive. In all honesty, the E7TE heads, such as this one, installed on 1987–1993 Mustangs aren't bad for stock pieces. Back when these cars were new, porting them was a great way to improve flow without forking out a ton of money.

33

First on the aftermarket cylinder head scene was Ford Motorsport SVO (now Ford Racing Performance Parts). Its early heads were cast iron, like the OEM pieces, but in 1995 it introduced aluminum versions, the Turbo Swirl and the GT-40X *(seen here)*. The latter is aimed at more modified street and street/strip engines, but both of them, like all of the GT-40 family, are among the most straightforward and rewarding to install.

GT-40X heads feature larger, 1.94-inch intake and 1.52-inch exhaust valves that really improve flow and, combined with aluminum construction, work especially well on mildly modified 302 engines. By comparison, the stock E7TE heads feature 1.78- and 1.45-inch-diameter intake and exhaust valves. Before installing your heads, get both the intake and exhaust sides ported by a machine shop, to improve flow.

replacement aftermarket heads have rendered porting the stockers all but superfluous.

In 1988, Ford Motorsport SVO (now Ford Racing Performance Parts) released its GT40 replacement iron heads (derived from those on the Le Mans–winning racers). These were similar in design to the 1960s originals and appeared after a proposed special 25th-anniversary Mustang with a hopped-up engine using these heads was scrapped.

As soon as they became available, enthusiast magazines fell all over themselves praising them, and enthusiasts snatched them up. Other manufacturers, notably Trick Flow and Edelbrock, quickly offered comparable designs. All three of these companies (and a few others) proliferated their offerings to include the street/strip and race end of things. The advantage was that the technology employed at serious racing levels eventually filtered down to the street.

When selecting heads for your street 5-liter (the race heads and serious street/strip pieces are really beyond our scope and deserve their own entry), bear in mind the kind of power levels your engine will be producing and whether it will feature power adders, cam and valve-train alterations, and displacement greater than stock.

Also make sure the heads are emissions compliant, as required for street cars by many states and Canadian provinces. (Compliant heads are likely to incorporate Thermactor air and exhaust crossover passages. These work in conjunction with your Mustang's EGR to recycle spent exhaust fumes and mix them with intake air, to keep the temperatures down and reduce the buildup of nitrogen oxides, or smog.)

The list of cylinder heads for 5.0 Mustangs is mind-boggling, and to keep things simple, we'll stick to the most popular and versatile heads available for street-going 5-liters. As a general rule, when installing new heads on a stock 302 short-block assembly, you don't want any heads with intake and exhaust valves bigger than 1.94/1.60 inches. Bigger valves are designed for forced induction and larger-displacement, higher-revving engines. They'll hurt torque on a naturally aspirated street engine, because the greater volume of air has nowhere to go, and you'll probably have to modify your pistons and change valve-train geometry (sometimes even the camshaft).

If you own a 1986 5-liter, pay special attention, because the factory heads and taller flattop pistons are a one-year-only deal. You'll need to change your factory pistons when you bolt on a set of replacement free-breathing stock or aftermarket heads (even those designed for pure street applications), to provide adequate valve-to-piston clearance and a pump-gas-friendly compression ratio.

If you're just starting out, two of the most popular replacement heads are the Edelbrock Performer 5.0 and the FRPP GT40. Trick Flow's Twisted Wedge (and their Street Heat predecessors) are also popular on street Mustangs but have slightly more specialist needs—they require specific valvetrain pieces and pistons (if an aggressive cam is installed) to exploit their full potential.

Beyond this, the Edelbrock Victor Jr.'s and other notable names, such as Brodix, Canfield, and Holley, are good and popular heads. However, these are aimed at serious street/strip and race applications, so their greater

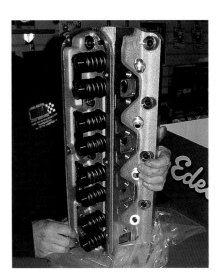

Another popular choice for a street 5-liter Mustang is Edelbrock Performer 5.0 heads. Aside from the GT-40, these are probably the best pure bolt-on heads available for these cars and are both affordable and of exceptional quality.

flow won't really benefit most street-going 5-liter Mustangs. Also, because they lack emissions provisions, they aren't street legal anyway.

Edelbrock Performer 5.0
Edelbrock heads are good-quality items that you can basically bolt on and forget about. The Performers are available only in aluminum, which reduces weight and is a better heat conductor than cast iron. This is great for 5-liter Mustangs, because it allows owners to run maximum advanced ignition timing. This makes them ideal for high-power normally aspirated and supercharged street cars that force greater than stock volumes of air into the combustion chambers.

These heads are available with 1.94- or 2.02-inch intake valves (see note above about maximum size for a stock engine) and 60 cc combustion chambers (versus 44 cc on stock E7TEs). Another nice thing about them is that they represent extremely good value and flow great right out of the box. They work especially well once you port the exhaust side—ha ha!

Ford Racing Performance Parts (Motorsport) GT40
These heads have been around for what seems like forever, but their staying power is testament to a sound, effective design that even today represents great value for money. Even more than the Edelbrock Performer 5.0s, these heads (made by FoMoCo) are bolt-in replacements for the stockers—install on a stock short block, and away you go.

The GT40s are available in three different guises, each of which suits some engines better than others. The orig-

inal cast-iron GT40s and the upstart GTP-40 still work well on fairly stock normally aspirated 5-liter engines, because they help boost power by retaining heat in the cylinders. The GTP-40 (derived from those used on V-8-powered second-generation Explorer SUVs) features improved combustion efficiency and is a solid foundation when building a powerful street 302. The downside is that it has different-sized exhaust valves than the rest of the GT40 family and requires special headers.

Ford also offers aluminum versions of these heads that are more beneficial for hi-po normally aspirated and supercharged applications—the Turbo Swirl (so named because of its high-swirl combustion chambers) and, for street/strip applications, the GT40X. This features bigger (1.94/1.52) intake/exhaust ports and is designed to work with FRPP's own line of upgraded camshafts and valvetrain hardware.

Airflow Research
Too few 5-liter enthusiasts know about AFR 165 cc aluminum heads, which are tremendous bolt-on pieces and feature a five-angle valve job plus CNC-machined intake and exhaust ports and combustion chambers straight from AFR. They make a great alternative to Trick Flow's hallowed Twisted Wedge heads, because they rival them for flow capacity but don't require fiddly valvetrain selection and adjustments. Another factor that makes them a good choice for a hi-po street 5.0 is that they are emissions legal.

You'll derive maximum benefit from your new heads by pairing them with an appropriate higher-performance intake manifold assembly. Buying these components at the same time allows you to match the two appropriately and fully exploit the flow characteristics of both to maximize power and torque. It also allows you to present both to your machine shop for match porting, should you decide to do so. (See Project 12 for more information regarding intake selection.)

Machine Shop 101
When installing replacement cylinder heads (and intake, for that matter), any porting and flow bench testing (recommended, even on street heads) should be done by a professional machine shop. Use one that has a good reputation, especially in the 5-liter Mustang market. Their expertise may cost you a bit more than some general machine shops, but the end result will be well worth it. Once you've got your ported and assembled heads back from the machine shop, you can begin removing your old heads and installing the new ones.

PROJECT 11 ★ *Removing the Engine and Installing Replacement Heads*

Time: 10 hours

Tools: Air pressure gun, floor jack, screwdrivers, wrenches, vise grips, adjustable torque wrenches, sockets, ball-peen hammer, breaker bar, engine hoist, chain or sling, engine stand, blocks of wood, scraper, plastic coating, acetone or similar solvent, pry bar, Sharpie marker and paper tags, two or more experienced helpers

Talent: ★★★★★

Applicable years: 1987–1995 (1986 needs to change pistons)

Parts: New heads, gaskets, bolts/head bolt kit, fasteners, fittings, quality gasket sealant

Tab: $1,000

Tip: Port match your heads, intake, and gaskets for maximum flow and power.

Performance Improvement: Improved exhaust flow, horsepower, torque, throttle response

Complementary Project: New intake manifold assembly and exhaust headers

You can tackle replacing the heads while the engine is in the car, but considering the size of the job and that you'll usually be replacing other components, such as intake and exhaust manifolds/headers, it's easier to remove the engine and perform the work with the motor on a stand. Doing it out of the car also means there aren't any clearance issues—things are less likely to get damaged, and the end result will be more satisfactory. When you're done, you can simply drop the completed engine back in the car, and ultimately, you'll probably save more time.

Make sure you're working indoors, such as a garage or shop, and that you have access to an engine hoist, jacks, and a lift, if possible. You'll also need a couple of friends to help you, because removing the engine and installing the heads can be tricky. If your Mustang has air conditioning, get a repair shop to discharge the system before you carry out any engine work.

Before you do anything, you and a friend should remove the hood, to provide adequate clearance. Clean the surface of the engine, to prevent any debris from getting in once you start taking things apart—a light hosing with an air gun is good for this. Remove the plastic intake duct that connects the air filter to the throttle body assembly, followed by the serpentine drive

Although you can install replacement heads with the engine in the car, it's easier to remove it for better access, especially because you'll often be replacing your intake and your exhaust headers too. You'll need an engine hoist and stand, plus a couple of helpful volunteers. If your 302 still has factory headers, like this one, you can attach the engine hoist chain to the hoist hooks. Removing the engine first also reduces the risk of any debris falling down the lifter valley or other critical areas when doing head work.

Once the motor is out, make sure it's secure on a stand. Taking off the distributor before you take the engine out of the car will save time when removing the intake to get at the heads, though you can still do this once it's on the stand.

Before installing your new heads, make sure the surface of the block is clean. Use a gasket scraper and solvent to make sure all the material has been removed. These engines are getting old, and the original seals are often brittle and can be tricky to remove.

belt and the exhaust H-pipe, along with the radiator shroud and clutch fan (on 1982–1993 models).

Drain the engine coolant (things will be exceedingly messy otherwise), disconnect the battery, and remove the distributor-to-coil wire before setting piston number 1 to top dead center (TDC), so you can remove the distributor. Set the piston position by using a big socket and a breaker bar on the vibration damper bolt at the front of the crank.

Mark the distributor housing below the number 1 spark plug wire terminal (the number for each wire is marked on it at the top, by the distributor), using a Sharpie. Pop off the distributor cap and rotate the crankshaft clockwise (from the front) until the mark on the vibration damper aligns with the pointer or TDC mark. If you're at top dead center on the compression stroke, the rotor will be directly opposite the number 1 plug terminal mark on the distributor housing If not, rotate the crankshaft another full turn.

Pull off the positive crankcase ventilation (PCV) and canister purge pipes and disconnect the throttle cable. Also disconnect the cruise control and automatic tranny linkages, if your Mustang has them. Mark and label the intake vacuum lines, then remove them.

Unplug the connector to the distributor and unfasten the bolt that secures the distributor. Disconnect and mark the spark plug wires before pulling the distributor off and stuffing the hole with a rag, to prevent foreign matter from getting inside the motor. Don't rotate the engine while the distributor is out, or the timing will be off, and you'll have to set it by viewing the valves.

Relieve the fuel system pressure (see Project 16), so you can disconnect the main and return fuel lines. Then disconnect the radiator, water pump, and heater hoses and the connectors for the engine temperature sending unit, throttle position sensor (TPS), exhaust gas recirculation (EGR) valve, and air temperature sensor. Mark all the lines to avoid confusion.

Remove the upper intake manifold and throttle body by undoing the six bolts that secure the upper intake to its lower counterpart. Place a rag or (even better) some plastic coating over the lower intake, to prevent debris from getting inside the motor.

It's time to remove the engine. Cover the fenders and cowl with a cover or some thick blankets, to prevent damaging them when pulling the motor out. Unbolt the power steering pump and air conditioning compressor (if the car has air) and place a jack under the transmission. Keep the power steering pump level, to prevent fluid leakage. If your Mustang is automatic, also remove the driveplate fasteners that link to the torque converter.

Move the engine hoist into position and attach a heavy-duty chain to the two engine hoist hooks (if the motor still has stock headers), or use a sling. Attach the sling or chain to the hoist and make sure it's tensioned. Remove the transmission-to-engine bolts and unbolt the motor mounts.

With a couple of colleagues helping, slowly maneuver the engine forward and up. Make sure the input shaft for the transmission is completely disengaged from the clutch (or that the torque converter is secured to the transmission on automatic cars—a pair of vise grips works well for this). Slowly bring the engine up and out of the car, being careful not to damage anything. Once

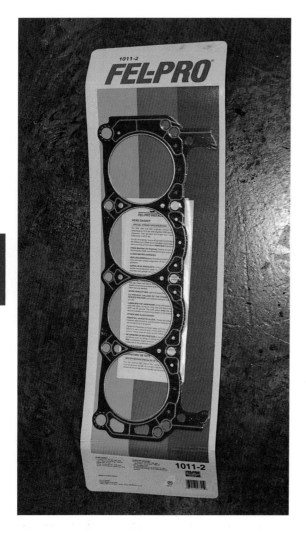

When replacing heads, choosing the right gasket is critical. Fel-Pro graphite gaskets, such as this one, are a great investment and are more than adequate for street engines. Copper gaskets are more suited to race applications.

it's clear, wheel an engine stand into place and secure the motor to it. Now the real work can begin.

Slowly turn and loosen the lower intake bolts until they can be removed by hand (turn them in quarter-turn increments). Then slowly pull off the lower intake. If you have problems getting it free from the block, use a pry bar and carefully pry the intake free. Cover the lifter valley before unbolting the exhaust headers, dipstick, and hoist hooks.

Slowly loosen the head bolts on one head at a time, carefully working from bolt to bolt in the same fashion as with the lower intake bolts, until you can twist them out by hand. When all of them are out, put them safely in a tray and count them, to make sure all are present. Lift off

Here are both of the new heads installed on a stock 302 short block, with the bolts ready to be torqued to spec. Make sure you start with the upper center bolts and work your way outward from the middle and that you gradually and properly torque the bolts. Overtorquing them will cause serious internal damage and warp the block and heads. Undertorquing them can also cause problems.

the cylinder heads and put them carefully aside. (If your old heads won't come off easily, put a piece of wood at the end of each of them and strike it with a hammer.)

Use a scraper to scrape away the old head gasket material until the block deck surface is clean, but don't abrade it to the point of damaging it. Use acetone or a similar compound to clean the surface. Remove the pushrods one at a time and place them in holes punched through an upside-down box in the same positions as in the head, so you can reinstall them in their original locations. (Draw an arrow on the box to indicate the front.)

Many new heads come with gaskets and bolts. If yours don't, you'll need to obtain them. When it comes to gaskets, graphite or copper are preferred. The former provide better sealing and water retention on street cars, while the latter are more effective on higher-horsepower engines. Make sure the gaskets correspond to the block and have holes in the same locations as the block (including the water jacket passages). Also note which way they go—most have a tab at the front that tells you.

For a mild street car with the stock block, use bolts rather than studs. Studs are usually longer and are designed for extreme and race applications, particularly on aftermarket blocks and for forced induction, where they provide a stronger seal between the block and heads to resist high-pressure exertion. On a factory block, these studs can do damage, by protruding into the water jacket passages.

You're best off—especially for aluminum heads—with a top-quality cylinder-head bolt kit, such as those avail-

Once the heads are in place and the sealant has set, install your valvetrain pieces. For fairly mild street engines, a set of aluminum 1.6:1 roller rockers, such as these Ford Racing pieces, work well with the stock pushrods and HO camshaft. The stock camshaft works surprisingly well for street and street/strip applications. It's quite possible to have a reliable 10-second Mustang using the factory bumpstick.

With its GT-40X heads and GT-40 intake installed, the engine is almost ready for final assembly and reinstallation. Even with pure bolt-ons like this, the performance gain is quite substantial—from 225 bhp to nearly 300 is quite the norm.

For maximum effectiveness, your new heads should be port matched to your new intake manifold. Port matching will provide a far smoother and thus more efficient passage for the air rushing from the lower intake into the cylinder heads and will add a bit more power. Match your new head and intake gaskets too (by grinding out material), to give a totally clean, unobstructed path for the air. As in the case of flow, every little bit helps.

Once your new heads are ready to be installed, make sure everything is clean on the surface of the block and that no debris has fallen down the cylinders or into the engine's internals (otherwise you'll have to completely disassemble the engine and clean the bare block). Use gasket sealer around the surface of the block before placing the gasket on top of it. Use more sealer on top of the gasket before installing the new head. After the head is on, carefully lube the bolt threads before installing the head bolts, making sure to only hand tighten them until all are in.

Once they're in, torque them to spec. Work with an experienced Mustang engine builder for this one if you have limited experience. Start with the upper middle bolt and work inside outward, torquing them gradually. When you begin installing the bolts, torque to 35 ft-lb, then to 50, then to 70 on the lower ones. On the upper ones, start at 35 ft-lb, then torque to 70, and finally 90.

When you're done, re-torque the middle bolts, so that the torque on the outer ones doesn't compromise their retaining ability and everything stays snug. Repeat the procedure for the other head.

Do note that these figures are for lubed bolts. Because torque wrenches get their measurement from the friction between the bolt threads and the hole threads, lubed bolts turn and stretch farther when torqued to the same reading. Lubed bolts should therefore be torqued to a lower setting than dry ones—65 percent is a general rule, but check with the fastener manufacturer where possible.

With the new heads installed, re-insert the pushrods in their holes, then install the intake manifold and rocker assemblies. Once you've done this, you can begin putting your engine back together.

able from ARP. Recommended by many experienced Mustang tuning shops, these offer an improvement in sealing over the inadequate stockers (crucial for modified engines). They'll also prevent you from overtorquing and thus deforming the cylinder bores and damaging your heads—a common problem on 302 HO blocks.

PROJECT 12 ★ *Installing a New Intake Assembly*

Time: 10 hours (removing the engine from the car)

Tools: Wrench, adjustable torque wrench, sockets, screwdriver, spring-lock coupler, ball-peen hammer, gasket removal solvent, blocks of wood

Talent: ★★★★

Applicable years: All (with focus on 1986–1995)

Parts: New intake, bolts, gasket, gasket sealer

Tab: $800

Tip: Port match your intake to your heads for best results and check/replace your thermostat.

Performance Improvement: More power, torque, efficiency, better throttle response

Complementary Project: Replacement heads and exhaust headers

I f you're already doing cylinder heads, you might as well upgrade the intake. The stock piece(s) were designed to work with the restrictive, stock cylinder heads. They'll prevent your replacement heads from obtaining the necessary flow and will consequently limit your overall increase in horsepower and torque. Also, you'll need to remove the lower intake manifold to get at the heads anyway. Carbureted cars use a different intake from the fuelie 5-liters.

Carbureted Intakes

Early 302s (1979 and 1982) had a heavy, restrictive, two-barrel cast-iron intake manifold. Things improved for 1983, when Ford introduced a new lower four-barrel manifold designed to work with the 575 cfm Holley carb. If you own an original two-barrel car, consider upgrading your intake and carburetor as one of the first things on your to-do list. (When you take off the original carb and intake, put them in a safe place if you want the option of returning the car to stock condition.) For all their improvements, the 1983–1985 four-barrel HO engines can benefit from an intake swap too.

Carbureted intakes for your 5.0 come in two basic categories—dual-plane and single-plane. Dual-plane intakes have a divided plenum for each bank of cylinders, with bilevel, or "dual-plane," runners. They're designed to improve power and torque from 0 to 6,000 rpm—the operating range for stock and mildly modified 5-liter Mustangs. These are the best choice for a basically street-driven car, because they'll enable you to exploit the engine's wonderful torque.

Single-plane intakes, which have a much bigger plenum and no divider, are designed to make top-end horsepower at the expense of torque and come into their own between 5,000 and 7,000 rpm. This makes them suited to serious street/strip and highly modified race engines.

One of the most popular replacement intakes on carbureted street cars is Edelbrock's evergreen dual-plane Performer intake. Its taller Performer RPM and even more radical Air Gap relatives are designed for more street/strip and race environments, for modified engines operating well above the stock 302's 6,250 rpm rev limit.

On sequential fuel injected 5-liter Mustangs, the stock intake assembly is fairly restrictive. The 1986 version, externally distinguished by the unique callout plaque with vertical lettering, is the most restrictive of all.

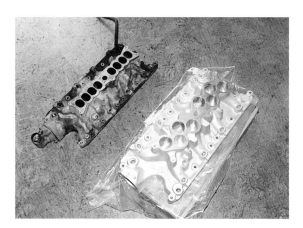

When it comes to replacement lower intakes, one of the original and best for street cars is still the Ford Racing Performance Parts GT40 intake. Compare it with the stock lower *(left)* and note the staggered cylindrical ports on the GT-40 version.

If you're installing your new lower intake on a basically stock engine, you can swap over your stock 19 lb/hr injectors and fuel rails, provided they're in good shape. Bigger injectors should be used only for seriously modified, nitrous, and supercharged applications, where the risk of detonation is greater and bigger fuel volumes are required.

Sequential Fuel Injected Intakes

Unlike carbureted intakes, fuelie manifolds only have to deal with flowing air, because the injectors squirt fuel into the combustion chambers. The stock SEFI 5-liter intake has two halves, an upper and lower, with long runners that help the engine generate its wonderful torque. Ultimately, however, like its carb predecessor, the stock fuelie intake is still a restriction, because it was designed to work within the confines of cost, emissions, and drivability.

Ford enlarged the upper intake for 1987, but it's still a choke point on your 5.0's engine. (If you have a 1986 5-liter, installing a factory 1987 upper intake will provide a noticeable increase in power and performance without any other modifications.) However, the aftermarket jumped on the bandwagon and now offers a plethora of replacements for the stocker. Below are some of the most effective and popular SEFI intakes for street 5-liter Mustangs.

Ford Racing Performance Parts GT40 Intake

Realizing that the intake was a major source of power restriction, early 5-liter tuners would hand port the bottom intake and use a saw to cut the top plenum from the upper intake runners, so they could hand port the runners. Then they'd weld the stock plenum and runners together again before bolting the upper back on the engine.

This was a crude, labor-intensive method that became redundant when Ford Motorsport (now FRPP) introduced its GT40 intake assembly. Like the stocker, it comes in two parts, but the lower intake features circular runners arranged in a staggered fashion, unlike the rectangular inline ones found on the stocker. The GT40 upper features formed, circular runners. Combined with the lower intake, this makes for a surprising increase in flow, thanks to less airflow resistance.

The only downside with the GT40 is that the design of the upper runners prohibits porting. For most owners who buy these intakes for their street 5-liter Mustangs, this isn't really a priority. Serious porting is designed to benefit highly modified engines that force considerably greater volumes of air into the combustion chambers than a stock 302. Like FRPP's cylinder heads, the GT40 intake remains a benchmark, despite the introduction of newer rivals.

FRPP Cobra Intake

Offering greater flexibility but still at a reasonable cost is the Ford Racing Performance Parts Cobra intake. As its name suggests, it's found on 1993 and—in modified form—1994–1995 Mustang Cobras. This is cast, unlike the formed upper GT40, and flows almost as well, thanks to a runner design similar to the GT40. Combining this upper with a port-matched GT40 lower results in considerable performance gains. The best part is that the Cobra intake upper runners can be ground out, providing enough flow for a big, bad supercharger.

Another advantage with the upper Cobra intake is that it doesn't require an EGR spacer when installing a bigger throttle body. The Cobra upper intake designed for the 1994–1995 5-liters also features a built-in elbow for the revised air intake assembly, whereas other brands require purchasing an "elbow" spacer to mate the intake pipe and throttle body with their upper manifolds.

41

One of the most popular replacement upper intakes for street 5-liters is FRPP's Cobra intake. This piece, in conjunction with a ported GT-40 lower, works surprisingly well and can support relatively large air volumes. These uppers are unique, in that they don't require a spacer, because they don't route engine coolant. Compare it with the stock 1987–1993 upper *(left)*.

Another popular choice is the Edelbrock Performer 5.0. These uppers were unusual in that you could unbolt the end to port the runners, instead of using a saw and welding apparatus to access them, as was necessary on other cast intakes during the early years of SEFI 5.0 tuning.

Edelbrock Performer 5.0, Performer RPM, and Performer RPM II

Another popular intake is the Edelbrock Performer 5.0, which flows better than the FRPP pieces yet is still an affordable, pure bolt-on proposition. It features a taller lower intake than the others and relocated upper-to-lower intake bolts (outside the airstream). It incorporates a large, 70 mm throttle-body orifice and will support significant power increases once you begin to do some serious hot rod tinkering on your 5.0's engine. It also allows you to remove the end of the plenum without sawing it off, to gain access to the runners. This makes it a natural for porting, once you start aiming for more impressive horsepower numbers. For best results, Edelbrock recommends you use this intake in conjunction with its 70 mm throttle body.

For more aggressive street cars requiring greater volumes of air (we're especially talking supercharged here), Edelbrock also offers its Performer RPM fuelie upper intake, with shorter runners and larger plenum, designed to boost power to 5,000 rpm and beyond while remaining street legal. The newer Performer RPM II is similar but employs a revised, triangular upper plenum. This provides yet more surface area for the air and serves to better distribute it and reduce turbulence as it enters the lower intake. Thus it improves breathing toward the top of the stock 5.0's power band.

Trick Flow

Also conceived for the street 5-liter crowd is the Trick Flow Street intake. A popular bolt-on, it's designed to maximize power through the stock 302's operating range (0–6,250 rpm) and works especially well once you port your heads and upgrade the valvetrain.

Fitting Your New Intake

When installing an aftermarket intake, you'll also need to select the correct injectors. For most street applications, you can simply swap over your stock 19 lb/hr injectors and fuel rails, because most lower fuelie intakes will have provisions for them. The stockers can support 300 horsepower without any problems.

Bigger injectors are best reserved for supercharged and nitrous applications and for naturally aspirated engines making power over 6,500 rpm, where air volumes are much greater, as is the risk of detonation. These applications thus need more fuel in a shorter amount of time, which they derive from higher-capacity injectors in conjunction with a bigger bore and shorter runners. Installing oversized injectors on your average mild street 5-liter will richen the mixture too much, causing erratic idling, drivability woes, and your Mustang to fail an emissions test.

When replacing or upgrading your intake assembly, especially if you're doing both the upper and lower, you'll need to remove your stock fuel rails and injectors from the lower manifold.

Depressurize the fuel system first (see Project 16). We'll also assume that you've already taken the engine out of the car and/or removed the intake manifold assembly. To take off the fuel rails, use a spring-lock coupler tool (available from most auto parts stores) to disconnect the crossover hose from the fuel rails. Then take out the four bolts that secure the rails to the lower intake.

Slowly pull the rails out. Once you're done, pull out the fuel injectors (rocking them gently from side to side) and examine them. Check for leaks and cracks. Examine

This Performer 5.0 intake is shown being installed on a 1988 LX. The spacer, throttle body, and EGR valve (the circular device at the back of the throttle body) are already attached.

the nozzles and O-rings and make sure the bottom caps are clean. If they aren't, replace the injectors.

Once the injectors have been checked and are found to be okay, carefully install them in the new intake manifold, so you can bolt your fuel rails back on and reconnect the crossover pipe. Always use new O-ring seals when replacing injectors or swapping them into your new lower manifold. Also swap over your thermostat housing, using a fresh gasket and quality sealer between the housing and your intake. The popular Fel-Pro gaskets are recommended for this and other areas (including head, valve covers, and intakes) on most street 5.0s.

Another tip before you put the intake assembly back together, as with your replacement heads, is to "match" the intake gasket to the runners on both your upper and lower intakes, grinding out material so the holes match exactly. This will further improve flow.

Extrude Honing

Besides porting, another great way to improve intake flow is by a process known as extrude honing. This involves pumping an abrasive putty through the runners to remove any imperfections and make the passageways smoother and more uniform. Each application can remove 0.1–0.4 inch of material. It improves not only flow but also efficiency, power balance, and combustion across all eight cylinders, reducing the chance of a particular cylinder running too rich or too lean. A really good idea is to port the intake first and then get it extrude honed afterward. The process may take a little longer, but, as the old adage goes, preparation is everything, and the results will be well worth it. Contact a good machine shop about this if you have limited experience.

Once your intake is ready to be installed (mount the heads first), examine the lifter valley of the block and the heads. Make sure all the old intake gasket material has been removed (to prevent leakage when you install a fresh gasket and the manifold). If not, use a scraper and some gasket removal solvent (available in cans from most auto parts stores). The contact surface should be clean, but don't abrade it too much.

Carefully reinstall the pushrods. Apply some RTV or equivalent gasket sealant (approximately 1/8-inch thick) to the surface of the block, where it mates with the intake and heads. Follow this with the gasket and some more sealant. Making sure everything is aligned, install the lower intake (the runners should be covered in plastic or rags to prevent debris getting in the engine). Install the intake bolts and carefully torque them to spec. (Install the intake on the lifter valley fairly rapidly, because the sealant will set in around 10 minutes. If you take too long, you'll have to do the whole process again.)

Now it's time to turn your attention to the upper intake and throttle body. In most cases you can just put the stocker away, but remove and keep the throttle-body-to-intake studs handy—you'll probably need them when installing a new throttle body on your upgraded intake. As mentioned previously, if you're using the popular Cobra 5.0 upper, you won't need a spacer between your 70 mm throttle body and EGR passages, because these intakes don't flow coolant through them. On all others, you'll need to install one.

If you're installing an aftermarket upper intake on your 1994–1995 5-liter Mustang (except FRPP Cobras), get an elbow adapter from someone like BBK, MAC, Edelbrock, or FRPP (the latter two are designed to mate specifically with each company's upper intake) to install an SN95 (1994–1995) 5-liter Mustang throttle body.

Once your upper and lower intakes have been prepped and or/ported, install your new upper on the lower manifold. The surface of your lower should be clean, so you can mount your new gasket and ensure a tight, leak-free seal. After the rags or plastic have been removed and the upper/lower gasket and sealant have been put in place, bolt on your upper intake and install and torque the bolts.

If you're going with a Cobra intake, remember when installing these uppers on the lower intake that you'll need two extra-long (7-inch) inner bolts to secure it, whereas on most other upper intakes you don't. If you're installing an Edelbrock Performer 5.0 intake, the bolts are in a different location compared with other intakes.

Bolt your throttle body onto the upper intake, using a spacer and gaskets if required, swap over your EGR valve (if it's still in good condition), and start putting everything else back on your trusty 302 motor.

PROJECT 13 ★ *Installing a Bigger-Bore Throttle Body and Mass Air Meter*

Time: 2 hours

Tools: Adjustable torque wrench, socket, wrench, screwdrivers

Talent: ★★★

Applicable years: 1986–1995

Parts: New throttle body, spacer (if required), gaskets, mass air meter

Tab: $300 (throttle body), $200 (mass air meter)

Tip: Keep your stock intake-to-throttle-body studs for reuse.

Performance Improvement: Improved airflow, horsepower, torque, throttle response

Complementary Project: New upper intake assembly and high-flow air filter

When choosing an intake, another aspect to consider is the throttle body (found on the right side of the upper intake) and a mass air meter to go with it. The stock 58 mm (1986) and 60 mm (1987–1995) throttle bodies pose another choking restriction on the 302's ability to breathe, so upgrading them is essential. Today, grinding out the stocker isn't really an economical way to go. You'll gain only an extra 3 mm in diameter, and out-of-the-box aftermarket throttle bodies flow far more.

A couple of things to remember: You don't want an oversized throttle body, especially on a normally aspirated car, because it will hurt torque, and therefore midrange power and drivability, rather than improving it. You also need to select a throttle body that's smaller than your mass air meter. Ideally, you want to create a gradual funnel effect for the air to increase the velocity as it passes from the filter through the cold air pipe and into the intake. For example, a 65 mm throttle body should be used in conjunction with a 70 mm mass air meter.

The 65 mm throttle body, again found on stock 1993 Mustang Cobras, is great for mildly modified street-going fuelie 5-liters. Particu-

larly when combined with the Cobra intake, it gives up no torque and drivability yet will support an engine making over 300 horses at the flywheel. BBK 65 and 70 mm throttle bodies are good and popular choices for street-going 5-liters.

You really shouldn't consider anything larger than 70 mm on a normally aspirated street Mustang, especially

When replacing your throttle body with the engine still in the car, remove your cold air intake pipe. If the vehicle is stock and has speed density metering *(like this one)*, ditch the pipe, because it doesn't have a provision for a mass air meter.

Choosing the right throttle body is as important as choosing the right intake. This 70mm BBK unit is perfectly mated with this Edelbrock Performer 5.0 intake. To fit the throttle body to the intake, you'll also need to source a spacer. BBK and other manufacturers supply these, but you'll often need to provide your own bolts.

if you're still running stock injectors. Torque will suffer too much, making your 5.0 decidedly less fun to drive. The 75 mm–plus biggies are designed for high-horse-power street/strip and race engines, where forcing a maximum amount of air into the combustion chambers is a top priority.

To install an aftermarket throttle body, unless you're going with a Cobra upper intake, you'll need to source an exhaust gas recirculation (EGR) spacer. Many aftermarket throttle bodies, such as the FRPP and BBK pieces, have corresponding spacers designed to mate with them and aftermarket intakes. In many cases, you'll also need to reuse your stock throttle-body-to-intake studs. Another good idea is to port match your throttle body and the corresponding gaskets and spacer to your upper intake as well, to maximize flow.

If you're removing the stock throttle body with the engine in the car, pull off the negative battery cable and remove the throttle position sensor (TPS) and throttle air bypass (TAB) connectors. Then pull the throttle body from the EGR spacer.

Swap over your stock EGR valve from the factory spacer to the aftermarket one on your new throttle body (unless you're using a Cobra intake, which doesn't require a spacer—the EGR simply bolts onto the back).

Use fresh gaskets between the new throttle body and spacer and intake, and make sure the surface is clean before you install the new gaskets. Swap over your EGR valve and hook up the TPS and TAB sensors, plus the PCV and heating/coolant hoses and EGR connectors (if you're doing this project on a street car).

Once you've taken care of the throttle body you can turn your attention to the mass air meter. Before you begin, you need to be aware of one very important thing: the type of air metering system employed on your 5-liter.

Speed Density

When Ford first introduced sequential electronic fuel injection on 5-liter Mustangs, they adopted speed density metering. This system works by having the engine's EEC-IV processor consult the throttle position sensor, manifold absolute pressure sensor, and oxygen sensors, then assume airflow and engine speed. With these as a guideline, the computer uses its internal programming to determine the optimum air/fuel ratio and required spark settings. It works fairly well on a stock 5-liter Mustang, but if you start performing any modifications to your engine, especially beyond heads, throttle body, and intake, it will cause idling and drivability problems. The system doesn't have the programming to compensate for airflow greatly increased beyond the stock parameters.

Mass Airflow

Beginning in 1988 on California-spec 5-liters (and then all of them from 1989 onward), Ford replaced its speed density setup with mass air. Unlike speed density, this system works by placing a hot-wire sensor directly in the

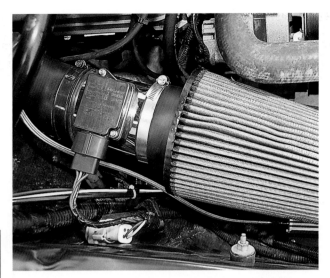

Shown here is a 75 mm mass air meter installed on a 1992 GT, along with a circular K&N FilterCharger Injection Performance Kit.

Performance Parts offers these conversion kits, which come with all the necessary hardware and software, including revised intake piping, connectors, and MAF EEC-IV processor ready to install (see Project 14).

Ford Racing Performance Parts 70 mm MAF Meter

When installing a replacement mass air meter, as with everything else, select one that corresponds to your engine's operating range, power output, and level of modifications. On mild, regular street 5-liters that came with a stock 55 mm MAF meter, stepping up to Ford Racing Performance Parts' 70 mm meter is a good idea. It slots right in place of the regular stocker, doesn't harm drivability, and can be tuned to work accurately with the fuel-injected 302's parameters, because it easily handles the air/fuel injector calibrations inside the Ford EEC-IV processor. It also enables Mustang owners to move up to larger, 24 lb/hr injectors without suffering any drivability problems.

Compared to most others on the market, however, it's still fairly restrictive and, working with a Cobra computer, it can retard ignition timing above 93 mph and between 3,700 and 4,200 rpm (around the limit on stock 302s for maximum torque and horsepower, respectively).

C&L Performance 76 mm

Another good vendor for replacement mass air meters is C&L Performance. Their replacement meters slide in place of the stocker and are bigger in diameter (76 mm and up). They alter (read increase) the voltage output of the factory hot-wire sensors by using bigger sampling tubes, which surround the sensors and hence increase airflow. These meters flow pretty well and allow you to step up to bigger injectors with few problems, but they aren't as accurate as the FRPP meters for calibrating with the stock EEC-IV processor. Therefore, they don't quite offer the same level of drivability.

Pro-M 77 mm

Beyond this level, Pro-M's 77 mm unit is also a popular choice and is basically a high-flow casting fitted with recalibrated factory hot-wire sensors. This also works fine on most modified, regularly street-driven 5-liters, but when you step up to bigger injectors, low-end torque and drivability can suffer. The reason is that only the voltage to the sensors is increased, while the EEC-IV computer looks at other parameters besides voltage to determine the correct/air fuel mixture, timing, and spark settings.

intake stream in the pipe between the air box and throttle body, to directly measure the volume of air coming into the engine. Another sensor directly measures the air's temperature. As a result, the mass airflow (MAF) EEC-IV processor can more accurately monitor airflow and compensate with more or less fuel, to achieve the desired air/fuel mix and operating parameters. This means that the mass air system is more accepting of performance modifications, because it can cope with greater-than-stock air and fuel volumes being forced into the engine.

The mass air systems in 1994–1995 5-liters are more restrictive. Although the meter is a bigger-diameter 70 mm unit, it incorporates a backflow inhibitor that reduces flow to little more than the 55 mm unit on the 1989–1993 cars.

These later 5-liter Mustangs are also restricted in that their EEC-IV and EEC-V (very late build cars) processors are more powerful, complex, and intelligent, allowing them to control more aspects of your 302's operation (a result of tightening emissions). For example, unlike the MAF sensors found in Fox cars, those on 1994–1995 Mustangs even allow the computer to check airflow at wide open throttle (WOT) and retard timing to achieve optimum fuel economy and emissions, thus reducing performance. The earlier Fox mass air cars simply default at WOT to timing data already programmed.

As you can see, if you own a 1986–1988 speed density 5-liter Mustang, you'll need to install a mass air conversion kit before you can fit your bigger MAF meter. Ford Racing

PROJECT 14 ★ *Installing a Mass Air Conversion Kit*

Time: 4 hours

Tools: Wrench, screwdrivers, tweezers, solder, drill

Talent: ★★★

Applicable years: 1986–1988

Parts: MAF computer, terminal, harness adapter, air intake pipe, mass air meter, MAF-compatible MAP sensor

Tab: $500

Tip: Make sure you also replace your MAP sensor.

Performance Improvement: Improved drivability, greater engine tuning flexibility

Complementary Project: Bigger upper intake and throttle body

As briefly outlined in Project 13, if you're planning on ultimately performing some serious modifications to your 1986–1988 5-liter Mustang's engine, you need to convert your engine's metering system from speed density to mass air. The reason is that the engine's electronic brain—the EEC-IV—uses very basic programming to monitor operating efficiency. It gathers data from the throttle position (TP), manifold absolute pressure (MAP), and oxygen (O_2) sensors to assume engine load. It then consults its internal programming (known as lookup tables) and adds more or less fuel to achieve the desired air/fuel mix of 14.7 parts of air to each part of fuel, which is optimum for fuel efficiency and emissions.

The problem with speed density is that it can't truly measure airflow accurately. As a result, the computer has to assume too much, because it doesn't have the programming to deal with the much greater than stock volumes of air coming into the engine. Therefore, it can't add fuel to compensate. If you upgrade beyond mild heads, a throttle body, and an intake, such as swapping in a different cam, your engine will suffer from continuous erratic idling and drivability problems.

Years ago, many hot rodders found Ford's new sequential fuel injection system a source of frustration. Many junked their early SEFI intakes and went back to carburetors. However, when Ford changed to mass air, beginning on 1988-spec California 5.0s, things changed forever. Although placing a MAF sensor (an obstruc-

tion) in the airflow path cost a few horsepower, the upside was improved drivability and engine electronics far more accepting of serious performance modifications. The system will compensate and still provide a smooth idle once you install a more aggressive camshaft, heads, and even a supercharger.

The mass air system places two sensors in the intake path: the mass airflow (MAF) sensor, to quantify the

Here are some of the major components that make up the Mass Air conversion kit. This modification is imperative on 1986–1988 speed density Mustangs if you wish to make substantial upgrades to your engine. Shown are a replacement MAF computer, mass air sensor, and the connector that attaches to it, incorporating the blue output, red positive, black negative, and brown ground wires.

47

On 5-liter Mustangs, the stock computer is housed under the passenger-side kick panel in front of the door. A simple snap tab holds the panel in place.

airflow, and the intake air temperature (IAT) sensor, to measure the air's temperature accurately. The EEC-IV measures the voltage required to keep the MAF sensor's "hot" wire (the one that measures flow) 200 degrees F above ambient, because the greater the voltage supplied, the greater the airflow. Many aftermarket mass air meters employ similar tactics.

The mass air conversion kit from Ford Racing Performance Parts comes with a new MAF-calibrated computer processor, replacement intake pipe with the MAF (meter and sensor) conversion wiring harness, wiring harness clips for the sensors and computer, and the required screws. Alternatively, you can try getting a used one from a wrecked 1989 or later 5.0—Mustang Parts Specialties is a good source for these (though remember that MAF computers on the 1990-and-up cars that came with airbags are different).

Installation is not too difficult, because the mass air kit is factory stuff, designed as an exact replacement for your speed density hardware. To do the job properly, however, take your Mustang to a shop that has specialized knowledge of these cars. If you're going to do the work and have limited experience, make sure somebody with considerable knowledge and wisdom about EEC-IV electronics is on hand at all times.

Under supervision, disconnect the battery and remove the passenger-side kick panel in front of door (it has a plastic tab that snaps it in place) to access the EEC-IV processor. Unplug the ports from your speed density computer that link it to the factory harness and remove it. The bigger one may require a 10 mm wrench to do it. Then you'll need a screwdriver to pull off the sleeve that covers the large connector, to expose the backpin. Pull out the large red locking insert with a small screwdriver and put it in a safe place.

Grab the connector and point the end toward you before pulling out wire number 50 and the two wires that control the Thermactor smog solenoids, 11 and 51. Get your

When installing a mass air conversion kit, you need to replace your speed density MAP sensor with one calibrated for mass air.

Because a mass air system can accurately measure airflow and compensate with the right amount of fuel, it works well on supercharged applications like this one.

MAF computer and put wire 11 into port 32 and wire 51 in port 38.

Bare the four wires on your new MAF sensor: output, ground, positive, and negative, and solder the MAF EEC-IV connectors onto them. Solder the blue (output) wire into port 50 of the MAF EEC-IV connector and the brown (ground) wire into number 9. Solder the red (positive) wire into the computer's number 37 main power slot and ground the black (negative) one with the tracer in port 40.

Then run a wire from the fuel pump monitor at port 19 to the fuel pump relay, under the driver's seat. The "hot" wire that comes out of the relay should be tan on an original installation; if it isn't, you have the wrong one.

Now direct your attention under the hood. Remove the plastic intake tract and install your new one with the mass airflow sensor attached. Install the mass air meter bracket at the front of the right shock tower.

Hook the four wire connectors on the MAF wiring harness to the MAF meter and mount on the bracket. Run the harness through the firewall to the interior. Pull out the factory engine management harness connector, located in the firewall. Drill a hole in it to run the MAF sensor's four wires through. Once you've installed them, push the connector back into its hole.

When installing the conversion kit, also make sure you swap your manifold absolute pressure sensor, located on the back of the firewall, for one calibrated to work with mass air, to prevent erratic idling and drivability problems.

Once everything is in place and you've had the installation checked by an experienced hand, reconnect the battery. The new hardware (and software) will look and perform as if it were fitted on the assembly line. Now you can really enjoy smooth idling and improved drivability and can begin hatching plans for some serious motor upgrades.

PROJECT 15 ★ *Installing a Supercharger*

Time: 48 hours

Tools: Adjustable torque wrench, sockets

Talent: ★★★★

Applicable years: 1986–1995

Parts: Complete supercharger installation kit

Tab: $2,000–$4,500

Tip: Do your heads, intake, and head gaskets beforehand, and make sure you have experienced help on hand at all times.

Performance Improvement: Improved horsepower, torque, acceleration

Complementary Project: Upgrade your cooling system

Of all the modifications performed to 5-liter Mustangs, installing a supercharger is probably the most well documented—and for good reason. A supercharger works by using a pulley driven by a belt off the crankshaft to turn a rotor that increases air pressure (boost) inside a specially designed housing. The increased air volume generated is then funneled into the engine's manifold, where it generates a serious increase in power and torque. On 1986-and-later 5-liter Mustangs, supercharger kits work particularly well.

Because sequential fuelie 302s separate the air and fuel paths, the blower can force a greater amount of air into the engine, and a recalibrated fuel system and bigger injectors (included with many kits) can compensate to achieve the right air/fuel ratio, without sacrificing drivability. Thus, unlike days of yore, you can have a 400–500-horse street machine that will idle nicely, and you can actually drive to work or the grocery store.

The only drawback with superchargers is price. Making serious horsepower costs money, and most blower kits start at around the $3,000 mark.

Selecting the right blower kit takes careful planning. Among the blower kits available for 5-liters, a few stand out—particularly for street cars, which is what most of us drive.

BBK Instacharger
If you have a stock or slightly modified 1986–1993 5-liter and you want to get into the supercharger game, BBK's Instacharger may be the blower for you. BBK teamed up with Eaton, manufacturer of OEM-style Roots blowers, to produce the positive-displacement Instacharger. Similar to the Eaton M90 installed on a number of factory production vehicles, the

Instacharger is a Roots twin-rotor design, using twin gear-turned lobed rotors to compress the air inside the casing. This design enables the blower to build up boost rather quickly, giving your engine a considerable wallop of satisfying off-the-line torque. It offers a neat, compact installation and will help a stock engine generate well over 300 fully streetable horsepower.

A great thing about these blowers is that BBK also supplies a ton of accessories with the Instacharger kit, including a bigger fuel pump, integral bypass and throttle body assemblies, a fuel management unit (FMU), underdrive accessory crank pulley, and spring-loaded belt tensioner.

BBK offers both 6- and 9-pound-per-square-inch (psi) boost applications. These blowers are best suited to pure street and occasional strip 5-liter Mustangs, because this Roots

A huge number of supercharger kits are available for 5-liter Mustangs, but for street cars, the most popular is probably the Vortech V-1 S-trim, due to its combination of fit, quality, reliability, and versatility.

Another great blower for street duty, especially considering that they now incorporate bypass valves and a ton of accessories, is a Kenne Bell twin-screw, like this one.

blower design restricts the amount of air you can force into the engine. You can't change pulleys to up the level of boost. They also tend to run hotter than others, because of an integral bypass that reduces air cooling efficiency. Therefore, to really make the most of the Instacharger, it's a good idea to install an air-to-water intercooler, to reduce the ambient air temperature.

Despite these drawbacks, the Instacharger represents tremendously good value when installed on a regularly driven street 5-liter. It's also fully emissions legal.

Kenne Bell

Similar to the BBK and M90, Kenne Bell superchargers are also positive displacement. However, the Kenne Bell blowers have a slightly different design. K-Bs feature two closely meshed twin-screw rotors, which improve efficiency compared to traditional lobed Roots designs and offer adjustable boost levels. For 5-liter applications, K-B offers its Whipplecharger 1500 and Blowzilla 2200 (the model numbers indicate their air capacity: 1.5 and 2.2 liters, respectively). They have the same size casing, but the latter incorporates redesigned, "deeper"-screw MX impellers, to produce even more boost.

Another advantage over many other superchargers is that K-B units are among the easiest to install. They bolt right on top of your lower intake and share the factory serpentine belt. Although these blowers developed an early reputation for causing detonation at greater engine load, this problem has been rectified with a bypass valve. Also, the company now makes them with a smoother inlet path and GT40 compatible upper intake manifold.

You can easily increase power output by changing the upper pulley. Although the K-B units are more expensive than some centrifugal superchargers (thanks to the specially made rotors and one-piece case), for entry-level buyers they still represent good overall value. Besides the ease of installation, they're among the most fun (the instant boost and throttle response are fantastic). Also, with up to about 18 psi boost available (in Blowzilla form), they'll suit around 90 percent of street and

Vortech kits often come with a fuel management unit. On entry-level blower kits, such as the company's V-1, the FMU adjusts fuel delivery so the engine receives the right amount of fuel, to compensate for the increase in air volume generated by the supercharger's spinning impeller. They plumb right into the stock fuel system, but upgrade your fuel pump too. A bigger replacement pump is usually included in most Vortech kits.

street/strip 5-liter applications. Like the BBK, K-B blowers are also fully emissions legal.

Vortech

The name Vortech is as synonymous with superchargers as Flowmaster is with exhaust on 5-liter Mustangs. This centrifugal blower (meaning that it uses a belt-driven impeller inside a circular, snail-shell-shaped housing to gradually build a centrifuge of air pressure, as opposed to the Roots and Kenne Bell units which use twin rotors inside a rectangular case) could support up to 10 psi boost. This enabled Mustang owners to fairly easily coax more than 450 horsepower without suffering breakage—a then common problem with these types of blowers, because of the freewheeling impeller-drive mechanism.

Not surprisingly it became a sellout success and paved the way for derivatives—the B- and R-trim blowers (the latter signifying race). The A-trim is still available but has been supplanted as the supercharger of choice by the S-trim. The S can reliably support up to 20 psi of boost, which translates into around 680 horsepower at the flywheel. It's considerably more efficient and cooler running than its predecessors.

Vortech kits come supplied with all the necessary ancillary pieces and fittings, for a top-quality (and reliable) installation. Also, the company sells virtually any accessory you could possibly need.

Installing Your Supercharger

Provided you have a decent amount of experience working on 5-liter Mustangs, there's no reason you can't tackle this project

When installing a supercharger, you'll need to replace your factory crank pulley. A billet piece, such as this one from Vortech, with provision for both the main serpentine and blower belt in front of it, is recommended. You can also get bottom blower pulleys that bolt onto the factory crank pulley—but if you're going this route and your car has underdrive pulleys, replace the crank piece for a Cobra item or stock pulley.

yourself. However, it would still be wise to do the work in conjunction with a specialist 5-liter Mustang shop, because installing a supercharger properly is quite fiddly. Therefore, this project is designed more as an overview than as a step-by-step guide to installing a supercharger, which is worth its own separate volume.

Our installation here will focus on the popular Vortech S-trim, as installed on a 1986–1993 Mustang.

Before you even begin, make sure you have experienced help, access to a shop or garage, the blower installation manual, and all the required tools and accessories. Below is a list of items you should have for a hassle-free installation.

Bypass Valve

The importance of this in conjunction with a blower cannot be stressed enough. The purpose of a bypass valve is to reroute hot boosted air via engine vacuum back to the blower's inlet side, to prevent boost backing up when the throttle butterfly is closed.

Bigger Injectors

An engine is basically a glorified air pump, but to make it run properly, you need to combine the right amount of air and fuel to achieve proper combustion. With a supercharger forcing a great deal more air into your 302, you need to compensate with bigger injectors and/or recalibrations to your fuel system.

However, you need to know how much power the various sizes of injectors will support. If you're making 276/332 horsepower (the latter is what you'll generally get installing a basic blower on an essentially stock engine) at the fuel pressure rate of 45/65 psi on a blown 302, the stock 19 lb/hr injectors will work fine. At the same pressure, 24 lb/hr injectors will support 349/418 horsepower, while 36

lb/hr units will work with 436/523 horsepower. Beyond this, still larger injectors are available, though they're really designed to work on radical race engines.

Fuel Management Units

When stepping up to larger injectors, you also need to consider fuel regulation. Most supercharger kits will come supplied with a fuel management unit that mechanically increases fuel pressure in response to rising boost, to help achieve a desired air/fuel ratio on blown engines. FMUs can compensate for the stock EEC-IV processor at wide open throttle, where the computer goes into default mode and isn't able to add sufficient fuel to match the volume of air being forced into the engine. FMUs are also able to override the stock fuel pressure regulator in response to boost.

Many individuals use FMUs with too-small injectors. This bumps up the fuel pressure too much and robs the injectors of power. Generally, you'll be looking at 12:1 (12 psi per pound of boost) calibration on your FMU for stock 19 lb/hr 5-liter injectors, 10:1 for 24–lb/hr, and 8:1 for 36 lb/hr injectors.

Pulleys

Some people switch to smaller pulleys, though you'll need a new belt if doing so. However using too small a pulley can increase inertia so much that it damages the blower's internal drive from excessive rpm. Also, installing smaller pulleys often voids the warranty on any supercharger.

Power Pipe

Most centrifugal street blowers will work fine with the intake tract supplied. However one item worth considering is Anderson Ford Motorsport's Power Pipe. This fits in place of the regular intake tract and harvests cooler, denser air from a filter inside the right fender, feeding it to the blower's inlet side via a large diameter mandrel bent tube. The result is improved throttle response and a considerable increase in top-end boost (up to 3 psi). It works especially well if you're aiming toward 10 psi boost.

Intercooler/Aftercooler

The cooler and denser the air going into your engine, the more power you can make. With superchargers generating a great deal of heat, you want to keep air temperature to a minimum. Thus using an intercooler, which acts like a radiator and cools the charged intake air, is well worth it, especially if you're shooting for 10 psi boost or more.

Several blower manufacturers also sell intercoolers to cool the charged intake air and add more horsepower. These are available in air-to-air, or air to water configurations. For the popular Vortech V1 street blowers, the company now sells its own Power Coolers to complement its blower kits. These are air-to-water intercoolers (often called aftercoolers) because they are fed ice and water, held in an underhood tank to cool the air's temperature, instead of doing it via a small radiator. The Power Coolers fit between the blower housing and intake manifold, thus cooling the intake air after it's been pressurized through the blower. Although they can be a little fiddly to install, they provide a fairly compact installation, plus they can add up to 40–50 horsepower.

Fuel Pump

As with a bypass valve, making sure you have the right fuel pump is critical. Installing bigger injectors and the supercharger hardware will be no good if you're still using your stock 88-liter-per-hour (lph) in-tank fuel pump. The greater volume of air, combined with stock fuel pressure, will cause a lean condition and detonation. For most applications, consider upgrading to a 190 lph in-tank pump.

Vortech usually supplies these with their supercharger kits. Although some people will go with a T-Rex or other inline booster pump, which boosts fuel pressure upstream of the new 190 lph in-tank fuel pump, this provides for a fussy installation and isn't really necessary once you upgrade your main pump. *Never* use a blower, T-Rex, and a stock 88 lph electric fuel pump together.

Brace

If you're aiming to make around 10 psi boost, it's also worthwhile to install a brace, which bolts to the supercharger accessory bracket and passenger-side exhaust header. This prevents the bracket from flexing under greater rpm/boost, which allows the blower belt to fly off, causing the supercharger pulley to freewheel and damage the impeller mechanism. On milder superchargers, the kit-supplied brace works fine.

Cooling System

Although this is covered elsewhere in this book as a separate topic, when installing a supercharger, your cooling system needs to be up to snuff. For 1986–1993 cars, consider a replacement aluminum radiator, electric cooling fan, and high-flow water pump your top priorities before beginning a blower install.

Ignition

Before beginning this project, make sure your Mustang has an upgraded ignition for best results with the supercharger. Vortech supplies MSD ignition components for its own blower kits, but whatever route you choose, your cap, rotor, plug wires, coil, and spark plugs should be new. It would also be wise to step up to an aftermarket ignition box, to better initiate the spark for the greater volume of air and fuel. When it comes to plugs, use colder ones than stock, but don't go with platinum-tipped ones.

Recommended for an additional horsepower boost is the Anderson Ford Motorsport Power Pipe. It gathers pressurized air from the inner fender and mixes it with the charged air from the blower before the latter enters the throttle body and intake.

Installing Your Blower

Once you have everything you need, you can begin the supercharger installation. Depressurize your fuel system and drain the engine of oil and coolant. Also change the oil filter. Take off the factory serpentine drive belt before disconnecting the negative battery cable. Unbolt the factory fan shroud and fan (if your car still has it), so you can pull them out.

Pull out the stock intake tract, MAF sensor, and panel filter and housing. Disconnect and mark all wiring and hoses to the throttle body. (If you have a 1986–1988 5-liter Mustang with speed density metering, convert to mass air before you begin—see Project 14.)

Turn your attention to the ground wire fastened to the radiator core support. Access the hole behind the right headlight and reroute the wire through it. Scrape away any paint, debris, or grease from the grounding point, to leave bare metal. Unfasten and pull off the upper radiator hose and the crankcase vent tube, which runs between the throttle body and oil filter, followed by the factory belt tensioner mechanism.

Unplug the wiring connectors that lead to the alternator and undo the bracket bolts. Pull the alternator off and put it aside. Remove the brace that links the Thermactor air pump with the engine timing cover. Now you can disconnect the air tubes to the pump and carefully pull it out.

Because the Vortech kit is fully emissions legal, you'll need to keep your rectangular-shaped emissions canister, on the right inner fender at the bottom, but relocated to provide sufficient clearance. Unbolt the bracket that attaches the canister to the frame rail and position it further forward, at an angle, by securing the front bolt into the rear bracket hole.

If you're running underdrive pulleys already on your Mustang, you'll need to switch back to a stock crank pulley before bolting on your lower blower pulley, or use a billet one-piece supercharger/crank pulley. The blower kit comes with longer washers and bolts to attach the blower pulley or billet

Growing in popularity on supercharged applications are intercoolers or aftercoolers. This Vortech air-to-water intercooler, also referred to as a powercooler or aftercooler, does just as its name suggests, cooling the compressed air (via ice and water stored in a resevoir) once it leaves the supercharger and before it enters the throttle body and intake. These power coolers can add up to 40 additional horsepower on a street S-trim blower kit.

aluminum piece to the crank pulley. Torque the bolts in a diagonal pattern, so as not to upset crank balance.

The Vortech and a lot of other centrifugal blowers require an oil feed, which you'll need to plumb into your engine's oil system. First mark a spot on the right side of the oil pan, toward the front at the top, then use a center punch to make a hole. (Be sure the pan surface around the hole is clean before you punch it through). The hole should be a maximum of 9/16 inch across.

Tap the hole with an NPT tap and cover the flutes on it with heavy-duty grease, to catch any metal fragments. Make sure the threads on the fitting are clean before dabbing them with silicone sealer, followed by the NPT hose with another dab of sealer. When the pipe is secure, make sure it's sealed all the way around; otherwise, oil will leak out.

You can now work on the oil feed line. Start by pulling out the oil pressure sending unit, on the left side of the block, and fitting the boss fitting for the line in place of it. Your supercharger kit will come with a nipple to be threaded into the block. Before putting it in, coat the threads with engine oil, then thread a tee onto the nipple and a 45-degree elbow onto the tee. Install your factory oil pressure sending unit into the end of the elbow.

You should have one remaining flare fitting, which should be threaded into the other hole of the tee. Hook up the red oil feed line to the back of the sender and route it up and behind the power steering/air conditioning compressor bracket. Cover the open end with a clean plastic bag to prevent any debris from getting in.

Now it's time to install your FMU. Move your stock relay, which is held in place by a screw, to the front of the right shock tower. Drill holes into the inner fender, in front of the shock tower, to secure the FMU and bracket with the sheetmetal screws provided. You'll need a special spring-lock tool to disconnect the fuel return line at the rubber hose (located on the right side of the engine).

Hook up the FMU inlet hose to the return line that feeds from the fuel pressure regulator (the inlet fitting is the external one on the left side of the FMU). Mate the FMU return hose (underneath) to the stock fuel pressure regulator. Secure the fuel lines using the tie wraps supplied, to prevent them from touching the passenger exhaust header. Mate the 32-inch hose with the fitting on top of the FMU, then link it to the B/R port, located on the multi-fitting on the driver's-side firewall.

Now that the oil feed and FMU are hooked up, you can begin installing the supercharger. Included with the kit is an accessory bracket, so you can mount the blower at the top, the Thermactor air pump below it, and the alternator at the bottom.

Note the length of the pivot boss on the alternator—it should be around 3 inches. Also measure the length of the boss on the air pump, so that if you have belt alignment problems, Vortech will be able to help you.

Mount the alternator and air pump on the bracket and push the retaining bolts through the rear of the bracket (mount the supplied tube spacer over the air pump bolt). You'll want to sandwich the air pump and alternator between the bracket and supercharger mounting plate, so you'll need to lower the plate over the bolts that secure the two accessories. Install the washers and nuts over the bolts but only hand tighten them. Fit the fastener right at the top of the mounting plate and install the two bolts that will attach the blower accessory bracket to the engine.

Mount your alternator brace, positioning it between the boss on the alternator and the air pump. If you're doing this on a 1992–1993 Mustang, you'll probably need to drill out the plugged hole in the air pump. Once everything is in place, torque and secure all the bolts and fasteners on the bracket assembly, before bolting it to the engine using the four bolts supplied. Hook up the alternator wires and use a tie wrap to fasten them securely.

With the bracket secured, you can tackle the air pump hoses. Remove the short and kinked hoses from the air control valve on the firewall. Reattach the short one to the diverter valve before linking it to the air control valve. Attach the kinked hose between the air pump and the air control valve (you might need to shorten the hose). Secure the hoses with the stock clamps and screws. Once your blower has been fitted, you may need to reroute the vacuum control line, but you can leave it where it is for now.

The supercharger will require greater effort from the cooling system, so you'll need to replace your standard upper radiator hose. The Vortech kit comes with a rigid stainless pipe that links two rubber stock-style hose ends. Cut a new stock hose in two, with one elbow longer than the other (it will tell you in the blower instruction booklet), then fit the rubber hoses over the stainless-steel pipe. The shorter rubber hose attaches to the thermostat housing, the longer one to the radiator. Make sure the seals and hose are secure.

Fit your factory belt tensioner to the mounting point on the supercharger accessory bracket. Swap the locknut for a regular one on the air conditioning compressor mounting bracket bolt by the water pump (if your car has air). You might also need to trim a little off the edge of the compressor mounting bracket, to clear the mount for your tensioner. The latter is designed to fit between the blower mounting bracket and the air conditioning compressor or power steering pump (non-A/C applications) bolt.

Now install your serpentine drive belt. Vortech kits usually come with one, but if yours doesn't, you can source replacement belts at most auto parts stores.

With the serpentine belt installed, mount the blower itself. Use a clamp screw to secure the critical oil drainage to the blower's drain fitting. Feed the hose from the fitting over the air pump and down to the fitting on the right side of the oil pan. Attach the blower to the bracket with the five supplied 3/8-16 x 1-inch bolts and corresponding washers. Use a hose clamp to attach the oil feed hose to the oil pan fitting.

At this stage, we're almost done, except for the blower belt, air filter assembly, and bypass valve. Beginning with the belt, fit the belt idler using the supplied bolts and washers, so you can slip the belt on. Then rotate the tensioner plate to gain the correct belt tension.

The boxy Vortech air filter cover goes where the stock panel filter element does, at the front of the right inner fender. Loosely place the cover in position before inserting your MAF sensor into the back of it, tightening the sensor housing with the clamp. Secure the air filter housing to the right inner fender with the supplied screws.

Vortech kits come with a rigid, molded 3-inch intake elbow and 3-inch flex tube to mate the air filter housing with the supercharger, though if you're using the Anderson Power Pipe, replace these items with the latter. The elbow and flex tube are secured by clamp screws. If you're going the Power Pipe route, Vortech supplies a special adapter sleeve and clamps to mate with it.

The bypass valve consists of a discharge tube, elbow, plumbing, the valve itself, and a connector that runs to the FMU. Fit the inlet elbow tube on top of the blower (facing downward). Install and clamp the supplied hoses on the valve at the two attachment points. Place the top bypass-valve hose fitting into the bottom of the metal discharge tube, which fits between the blower and throttle body. Splice the vacuum line for the bypass valve into the FMU line, using the tee and vacuum line supplied.

Your supercharger installation is now complete. Before going any further, check the lines carefully for leaks, especially fuel

A step up from the basic V-1 is this S-trim installation with all the goodies, including a Power Pipe and aftercooler. With the addition of mainly bolt-on pieces, including heads and intake, but a stock 302 block, this combination turned an astonishing 589 horsepower to the rear wheels on a chassis dyno.

and oil, and make sure all the wiring is safe and away from anything that could damage it. Have an experienced installer go through it with you.

If you're running advanced timing, back it off to around 10 degrees before top dead center (BTDC) to reduce the risk of detonation. If you haven't already, change your stock spark plugs for colder ones. These blowers require you to run 92 octane fuel or higher, but retarding the timing and changing the plugs will enable you to run 91 (the highest grade available in many areas) without pinging. It also saves you having to buy octane booster all the time.

Refill the engine with fresh coolant and oil, and check the belt tension. If everything is okay, hook up the battery, fire up the engine, and let it run for a few minutes. Check the installation and look for any leaks. Shut it off and let the engine cool a little. If everything is okay, fire up the car and go for a drive with an experienced installer. If all is well, the difference in performance before and after the blower install will be like night and day.

Boost Controller

One thing you might want to consider with Vortech blowers is an adjustable boost controller. This enables you to retard the ignition setting in response to boost, to compensate for changes in altitude, air density, and fuel quality, to achieve optimum performance and reliability. Installation is fairly simple, in that the controller is prewired. All you need to do is plug the adapter into the coil in place of the stock connector harness and link the latter to the adapter.

Mount the box that houses the boost controller and ground the black wire. One of the best places to mount the box is in the left inner fender, after relocating the battery to the trunk (Project 37). The controller comes with a special tee and hose. You'll need to splice into the tube from the vent on the controller to the FMU vacuum/fuel hose.

Install the knob for adjusting the ignition on the dash or console inside the Mustang, and route the wires through the firewall. All you then need to do is insert the wires into the connector on the boost control unit.

For each pound of boost the blower generates, the controller is adjustable from 0–3 degrees of ignition retard. When retarding ignition, though, make sure you work with someone experienced in Mustang superchargers for best results.

PROJECT 16 ★ *Replacing the Fuel Pump*

Time: 2 hours

Tools: Adjustable torque wrench, floor jack, block of wood, 13 mm socket, brass punch, hammer, solvent/cleaner

Talent: ★★

Applicable years: 1984–1995

Parts: New pump and lock-ring gasket

Tab: $80–$200

Tip: Make sure the gas tank is almost empty before you begin.

Performance Improvement: Improved fuel flow, engine longevity, throttle response

The fuel system is one of the most overlooked areas affecting performance. In particular, the stock fuel pump on SEFI cars—an underachiever at best—often causes problems after a few years and needs replacing. During the course of its long life, the 5-liter Mustang came with three different styles of fuel pump. Carbureted cars have a pump mounted on the block and driven off the camshaft. Early central fuel injected (CFI) models had two electric pumps—a low-pressure one inside the fuel tank and a high-pressure one mounted on the chassis. When the 5.0 went to sequential fuel injection, a single high-pressure pump inside the tank replaced these, and that was the way things stayed until 1995.

The mechanical pumps operate under fairly low pressure (6–8 psi) and by their nature are generally reliable. Their only downside is that they rob the engine of horsepower, because they require a sizable amount of energy to run. The electric fuel pumps are an entirely different story. They don't rob the engine of horsepower. But because they operate at much higher pressure (39 psi on CFI applications and as much as 45 psi on SEFI systems) and are electrical, they're more likely to cause problems. SEFI pumps are factory-rated at 88 lb/hr but frequently deliver less than that, especially as your Mustang gets older. (Keeping the tank closer to full than empty will increase pump life.) If you can hear your in-tank pump whining noisily at idle, it's probably time to replace it.

Another good way to find out if your pump needs replacing is to check operating fuel pressure at the Schrader valve, mounted on the fuel rail by the intake. A third way is to disconnect the wiring harness from the pump and install a jumper between the pump and the battery. If you can't hear the pump operating, it's toast.

Before replacing an electric fuel pump, the fuel system must be depressurized; otherwise gasoline will spray all over the place when you start fiddling. The "inertia switch"—a safety device that shuts off fuel to the engine in case of an accident—provides a quick way to do this. Jack the car up and support it on axle stands or (preferably) a lift. Locate the inertia switch —under the left trunk hinge by the inner fender on coupe and convertible Mustangs or by the lid lock mechanism on hatchback cars. It's usually hidden under a portion of the

Fuel pumps on SEFI 5-liter Mustangs weren't too great from the factory, and probably need replacing after 10 years or so. If your engine is still mainly stock, swapping out the weak 88 lph pump for a 110 lph replacement like this one is a cheap and wise investment.

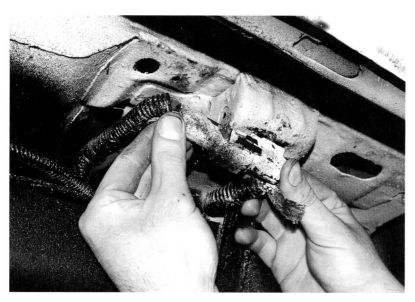

Because the fuel system is under high pressure on SEFI cars, depressurize it before beginning work by pulling out the electrical connector on the inertia switch and running the engine till it stops.

lines. Now you can completely lower the tank and move it out of the way.

Caution: When working on the gas tank or fuel pump, do it in an area far from any combustible materials, including sparks, open flames, or gas boilers.

With the tank removed, use a dowel or soft brass punch (not steel, which could cause a spark) to tap the lock on the fuel pump/sending unit counterclockwise, until you can pull it out. Carefully ease the pump assembly out of the tank, along with the old lock-ring gasket. This is also a good time to appraise your tank's condition. If it's starting to fall prey to rust, you'll want to replace it now. Stick with replacement rather than repair, because most gas tank sealer repairs are marginal at best.

trunk carpeting or the plastic interior trim. Pull out the electrical connector, then start the engine and run it until it stops (this should take just a few seconds). When it does, the fuel system is relieved of pressure, and you can begin work.

If you're replacing the in-tank pump (as will be the case on most 5.0s), remove the gas tank from the frame. Before you begin, make sure the tank is almost empty, which will make it easier and safer to maneuver around the shop and will mean less gas to siphon out, which will save you a ton of time. When siphoning the tank on a CFI or SEFI car, you may have to move the siphoning tube around to get all the fuel—the tanks in these cars incorporate reservoirs near the pickup point that keep the pump supplied when the fuel level is low and the Mustang is cornering. Once you're done, disconnect the negative battery cable under the hood and undo the filler neck bracket bolt before pulling off the filler and breather tube.

Pull out the pump and sending-unit harness retaining clips using a screwdriver. Position a jack on the floor, under the center of the tank, and place a block of wood on top of it. Raise the jack until it supports the bottom of the fuel tank. Remove the bolts at the front of the fuel tank straps with a 13 mm socket and an impact wrench. Gently lower the jack. The tank should drop at the front—the straps are hinged at the back and can be swung out of the way. Lower the tank enough to remove the wiring harness and disconnect the fuel and vapor

Make sure you choose the right pump for your engine. Although bigger is better for many applications, this isn't always so when it comes to your Mustang's fuel system. If you have a stock 302, installing a monster 255 lph pump will cause more harm than good, because the engine can't use all the fuel the pump is trying to send. The fuel system and regulator won't be able to cope, and you'll get frictional loss, fuel heating, and greater line pressure, putting tremendous strain on the fuel system, even at low rpm.

If your Mustang is basically stock, consider going with a 110 lph replacement pump, such as those available from Carter/Federal Mogul. These will improve fuel delivery over the factory pump yet still operate in harmony with the rest of the fuel system. For more aggressive street/strip cars, including those running bigger-than-stock injectors, fuel management units, and forced induction, a 190 lph unit, available from Ford Racing Performance Parts and other vendors, will be more than sufficient, even if your car is already making over 400 horses.

When you're making this amount of power and using forced induction, many 5.0 owners use an inline booster fuel pump, such as Vortech's T-Rex, and a larger fuel line between the two pumps. The inline pump is designed to supplement the chores of the in tank pump, by boosting line pressure and increasing flow from the tank forcing the fuel upstream at increased pressure so a modified

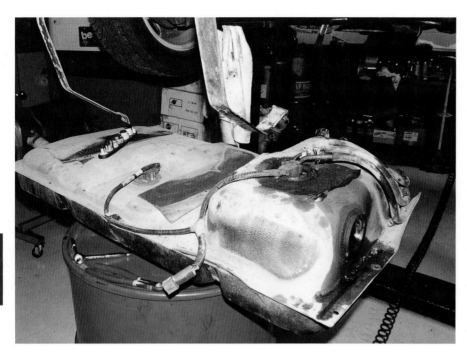

Accessing the fuel pump requires dropping the fuel tank from the frame. It's held in place by two steel straps, secured with 13 mm bolts. Use a jack or something else, like this drum, to support the tank when undoing the straps and lowering the tank. The pump and sending unit are on the right side of the tank, at the top.

are designed to work with highly modified engines that feature bigger injectors, larger lines, and over 500 horsepower. For these applications the big pumps are exceptionally durable and can meet the demands of flow and pressure, especially on engines with serious forced induction. They also require much greater voltage, so a heavy-duty alternator and battery are mandatory.

Once you've selected your pump, remove the main- and return-line electrical connectors before removing the old pump from its brace. Clean the tank mounting surface, fuel pump flange, and seal ring groove. With your finger, dab some

engine isn't starved of juice. Installing larger lines between the in-tank and booster pumps theoretically reduces the chance of fuel surge.

However, Joe Da Silva, of Da Silva Racing, doesn't recommend a booster pump in most cases. He says, "For all but the most extreme street and strip/race applications, where you're making 500 horses, a 190 in-tank pump is the way to go. The problem with the booster pumps is that they add complexity. Many people try to use them in conjunction with the stock in-tank, which they suck dry, eventually causing the stock pump to fail. However, the booster pump is still forcing fuel through the system, so you don't know which pump has failed. For ninety percent of the cars we build and service, a 190 is more than sufficient. We've dynoed up to 466 horsepower at the rear wheels using the stock fuel lines and a 190 in-tank with no problems, so really there isn't a need for a booster or even larger-than-stock fuel lines, unless you're making major power. But then you'll be running a fully modified fuel system anyway."

The big 255-lph-and-larger in-tank and external pumps, such as those from Paxton and Weldon Racing,

heavy grease on your new lock-ring gasket to keep it in place, then install and securely fasten the fuel pump assembly and gasket.

Reattach the gas tank to your Mustang's frame, carefully retracing your steps to install the wiring harness, sending unit retaining clips, tank straps, filler neck, breather tube, and fuel and vapor lines. When you're done, remember to refill the tank with fuel before starting the engine.

If you have a CFI car and need to replace the chassis rail pump, depressurize the fuel system, then remove the outlet and inlet fuel lines to the pump, along with the electrical connectors to the body harness. Remove the pump by bending the tab and sliding it out of the retainer. Pull the electrical wiring harness from the pump assembly by placing a screwdriver between the connector and retainer clip and moving the connector toward the pump inlet.

When installing the new pump, use fresh gaskets and seals on the fittings. Also make sure the electrical connectors are installed tightly enough that the boots seal and that the tabs and brackets don't touch the pump, because they'll cause a short.

PROJECT 17 ★ *Installing a Nitrous Kit*

Time: 4 hours

Tools: Wrench, adjustable torque wrench, sockets, screwdrivers, drill, portable MIG welder

Talent: ★★★

Applicable years: 1986–1995

Parts: Nitrous bottle, nitrous management unit, brackcts, screws, braided lines, jets and fittings (complete kit)

Tab: $80–$200

Tip: Mount the bottle before delving under the hood.

Performance Improvement: Improved exhaust flow, horsepower, torque, throttle response

Complementary Project: Upgrade your ignition and, especially, use colder spark plugs

Besides installing a supercharger, bolting on a nitrous oxide kit is one of the most talked-about topics when it comes to 5-liter Mustangs. This special chemical compound, N_2O, gives you an extra shot of oats on demand, without having to build a complete hot rod engine or install a supercharger. You can plumb in your nitrous kit, turn on the bottle, and hit the switch at the track, then turn it off to drive home and back and forth to work.

Nitrous is attractive because it costs a lot less than installing a supercharger or building your motor up and doesn't give up any power, drivability, or fuel economy. However, nitrous has its downsides, too. Most systems can't be operated on the street, because of state or provincial requirements. Also, in many cases, installing a nitrous system has caused the engine to blow up or the car to catch fire. If you've gone to the drags and watched Mustangs race, you've probably seen something like this at least once. Therefore, when considering a nitrous install, tread with extreme care and select the kit that's right for you.

How It Works

Oxygen represents about 21 percent air but about 36 percent of a nitrous oxide molecule. Nitrous oxide is stored under pressure, to keep it liquid. This liquid rapidly expands into a gas upon release—usually upstream of the carburetor or throttle body—and absorbs a large amount of heat, providing a dense, cool charge of oxygen. This dense, cool air rushing into the engine allows it to burn more fuel and produce more power.

Wet versus Dry

This is a hot topic in the world of nitrous systems. The wet setup uses two solenoids—one for the nitrous and one for the fuel, both of which are sprayed into the engine's intake assembly at the same time. A dry system, designed for sequential fuel injected engines only, uses a single solenoid for the nitrous. A second line connects the nitrous bottle and the fuel pressure regulator. Pressure from the bottle boosts fuel-line pressure, which richens the air/fuel mixture to boost power and ward off detonation.

Nitrous kits come in many forms, but for 5-liter Mustang enthusiasts on a budget, one of the best choices is the one from ZEX. Traditional nitrous kits are usually fiddly to install, because of all the separate solenoids and wiring, but ZEX takes the pain out of this by incorporating most of the hardware in a single box, the nitrous management unit (NMU). *Evan Smith*

Probably the best place to start is with the nitrous bottle itself. The right side of the trunk or hatch area is a good location, because it helps weight distribution by placing greater mass over the rear of the car, thus aiding traction and hookup when launching at the track. *Evan Smith*

Drill a hole in the factory intake ducting for the nitrous spray nozzle. For maximum results, the best place is right in front of the throttle body, as shown here. *Evan Smith*

What are pluses and minuses of wet versus dry systems? The latter are emissions certified by the California Air Resources Board (CARB) for 75 and 150 horsepower but cannot support more than that, because they use the stock fuel system. Wet systems can support far bigger horsepower numbers while still being emissions friendly, but if you install one on a sequential fuel injected Mustang, poor fuel atomization will cause puddling, backfires, and even more serious internal engine problems (some Mustangs have even burned). Therefore, on most street and injected 5-liters, consider going with a dry system, while on more street/strip and carbureted applications, a wet system is the way to go.

Nitrous Oxide Systems (NOS) and, more recently ZEX, are among the top vendors for dry systems. The latter is particularly good for 5-liter owners who regularly drive their cars and just want a little extra zoom at the track. It's also one of the easiest kits to install.

Installation

Because most 5-liter Mustangs are getting on in years, a few important aspects must be considered before performing a nitrous install. The first concerns the mileage and condition of the engine. The stock 5-liter HO, with its heavy-duty internals, will put up with a lot of abuse, thanks to small crank journals, a short stroke, and a stock roller camshaft (on 1985-and-up models). However, if the engine has never been apart and didn't receive regular maintenance, it's probably not a good idea to plumb in a nitrous system. Nitrous is an amplifier that boosts engine power and torque but will also increase the chance of serious engine damage.

The risk of damage increases with the amount of nitrous you're forcing into the engine. On a regularly driven Mustang with a stock 302, you shouldn't really consider more than a 100-horsepower shot. Anything more and you run the risk of blown head gaskets, detonation, bent valves and rods, and other serious problems. Some owners install 150-horse dry systems on their weary stock fuelie Mustangs, but in most cases, it isn't long before their engines give up the ghost. Some people will also try to use nitrous in conjunction with a blower or turbocharger on their street cars, though this isn't recommended for pure street 5-liters (go with a single power adder) unless you like uncontrollable driving characteristics and frequent engine rebuilds.

When it comes to nitrous oxide for 5-liter beginners, not only is the ZEX kit easy to install, but the activation switch, solenoid, and wiring are contained in a single box, called the nitrous management unit (NMU). This enables you to complete the installation in less than half the time of other systems. All you need to do is plumb into the throttle body, hook up a few wires, and install the nitrous bottle in the trunk.

Nitrous is often associated with blown engines because of a lean condition—too little fuel and too much oxygen. The ZEX system's NMU is great because, once you've armed the system via the toggle switch, it uses signals from the throttle position sensor to control the nitrous solenoid. The system can constantly adjust the ratio of nitrous to fuel, to maximize performance and minimize the risk of detonation. It does this by bleeding off a small amount of pressure to the NMU, so that the latter has an accurate reading of bottle pressure at all times. Therefore you'll always have the correct

Once the hole has been made, plumb in your nozzle and hook up the piping to your NMU. After installation, you can change the size of the jets to increase or decrease the amount of nitrous. *Evan Smith*

white wire that runs from the NMU to the voltage output wire that mates with the factory throttle position sensor. Ground the black wire and install the arming switch for the nitrous system to the NMU and harness. Some people choose to install nitrous switches in the ashtray receptacle on their 1987–1993 Mustangs, but a better location is on the console, right in front of the center armrest.

Activate the system by flipping the arming switch and turning the ignition key on. Keep the throttle open for a few seconds. If all is well, the light on the NMU should change from green to red, indicating that it has learned the change in voltage from the factory throttle position sensor.

Before using the spray, two more steps are required. First, cycle the arming switch, after which the light on the NMU should turn green. Open the throttle again and listen for the solenoid. If you hear it clicking, all is well. Second, retard your engine's ignition timing (if it's been advanced), to avoid detonation. Use a timing gun and twist the distributor back to between 8 and 10 degrees before top dead center. If your spark plugs haven't been changed, now is a good time to do it. Switch to colder, shorter spark plugs.

You'll need to run high-octane fuel when using nitrous—try Sunoco Ultra 94 if you can get it, and don't use anything under 91. At the track, if you can get only the latter, add some octane booster as a further defense against detonation.

Nitrous can be great fun, but it also poses the risks of damage and fire mentioned. Be sure you read and understand all the manufacturer's documentation. Also buy a fire extinguisher and mount it in your car, where you have ready access to it. A good place is on the floor, just between the glove box and the front passenger seat.

Test your nitrous setup at the track, giving yourself plenty of room to accommodate the rush of power. If you're starting with a small shot—50 or 75 horsepower—and wish to increase it, you can do this by swapping the nitrous jet in front of the throttle body and the fuel jet that hooks up to the NMU. But remember, you shouldn't use more than a 100-horsepower shot consistently on a stock 5-liter engine if you don't want things to break.

amount of fuel flowing through the system as it compensates for high or low pressure.

To begin installation, pop the trunk and pull up the carpet, so you can install the bolts and attach the bottle brackets. (Always install the bottle on the right side of the trunk if you can, so that it aids weight distribution.) Once the bolts are installed, lay the carpet over them, but punch small holes, so you can bolt the brackets to them. When they're secure, you can install the nitrous bottle.

With the bottle in place, run the braided line supplied in the kit from the trunk to the engine compartment. A good way is to drill a hole in the floorpan just behind the rear seat. Secure the line on the right side of the passenger compartment, hiding it under the plastic trim. Then run it through the hole and up to the right inner fender.

A good place to put the NMU is on the right inner fender, behind the air box assembly. Here it can easily mate with the nitrous bottle supply line and is also in close proximity to the throttle body. Follow the instructions in the kit by drilling four small holes in the fender and fitting the NMU backing plate over them before installing the bolts.

Once everything is in place, drill and tap a hole for the nitrous jet at the top of the plastic intake sleeve, right before the throttle body. Screw in the nitrous spray nozzle, hook up the jet, and connect the nitrous line to the jet and NMU. Hook up the fuel jet and line between the NMU and fuel pressure regulator. Then connect the

PROJECT 18 ★ *Upgrading the Cooling System*

ENGINE

Time: 4 hours

Tools: Wrench, adjustable torque wrench, impact gun, sockets, screwdrivers, drill

Talent: ★★★

Applicable years: All

Parts: Radiator, spring cap, fan (1979–1993), hoses, thermostat, water pump, coolant, oil cooler

Tab: $200–$950

Tip: Upgrade the entire cooling system if you're planning on extracting more than stock horsepower/torque levels.

Performance Improvement: Improved performance, engine cooling, longevity/reliability

Complementary Project: Transmission cooler (on automatic transmissions)

This project is designed more as an overview than as a specific task, since you should upgrade more than one aspect of your cooling system.

Radiator

The stock brass/copper two-core radiator found on 1979–1993 Mustangs is good at what it does, but over time, extended attack from road debris can damage the cooling fins. Eventually they can break off. Also, if the coolant incorporates mineral water and hasn't been changed frequently, scale builds up and coats the surface, compromising its ability to transfer heat properly. This is a particular problem on Mustangs with automatic transmissions, because part of the radiator doubles as a tranny cooler, putting extra strain on the cooling system.

Unlike the old days, you can't refurbish your radiator but instead must purchase a new one. If you're driving a stock, normally aspirated 5-liter and are on a budget (as many of us are), a good and fairly cheap way to upgrade is to install a slightly thicker, three-core brass radiator and mate it with the stock radiator shroud and clutch fan.

If you're modifying your engine and installing a supercharger (and therefore generating a large amount of heat), an aluminum radiator is the only way to go. Not only is aluminum a far better conductor of heat, but the lighter mass permits a radiator with much larger end tubes than its brass counterpart, offering far greater cooling ability and much less weight. Welding the end tubes to the radiator instead of soldering them also improves heat conduction.

Thermostat

The thermostat controls the flow of coolant in and out of the engine. On start-up, the thermostat is closed, to prevent coolant flowing through the radiator. As the engine reaches its normal operating temperature, the thermostat opens to allow the now hot coolant in the engine's water-jacket passages to return to the radiator, which cools it. Stock thermostats on 5-liter Mustangs run at 192 degrees Fahrenheit.

This stock radiator is still in fairly good shape, but you can see the buildup of scale between the cooling fins.

Besides the radiator, another cooling system component that should be on your attention list is the water pump. The stock pump is amazingly reliable, but for modified engines, you'll want an aftermarket piece that flows even better, such as this aluminum one.

Over time, the thermostat can stick open or closed, causing the engine to take a long time to warm up (stuck open) or overheat (stuck closed). If you've just purchased a Mustang with a few modifications, it would be wise to check what kind of thermostat is in it. When the sequential fuelie 302 debuted for 1986, hot rodders swapped the stock thermostat for a cooler 160-degree unit, to reduce coolant temperature and boost power. However, this isn't recommended on an EEC-IV-equipped pony.

Also, on Mustangs equipped with the EEC-IV, installing a 160-degree thermostat triggers the computer to remain in open loop and thus artificially richen the air/fuel mixture too much, which hurts fuel economy, drivability, and emissions and will ultimately increase engine wear. For most applications the stock thermostat will work fine, although if you live in a hot climate (90 degrees plus), and especially if you're running a supercharger or high-horsepower engine that requires greater volumes of air and fuel, consider a 180-degree unit.

Hoses

To keep the cooling system functioning properly, your hoses must be in top shape. The stock rubber hoses on 5-liters become brittle after a few years.

If you want to upgrade your hoses (a good idea), you can purchase the silicone pieces originally fitted to Special Service Package (SSP) Mustangs or those originally sold in the Middle East (OPEC). Another solution can be found in quality aftermarket pieces, such as the multicolored items made by Samco Sport and widely available through auto parts stores and speed shops. These are also constructed from silicone but seem to last longer than the regular SSP items.

This view shows the stock plastic fan and clutch found on 1982–1993 V-8 Mustangs. In good order it does a sterling job and will even work well on mild supercharged street applications like this.

Fan

On stock 5-liter Mustangs, and we're particularly referring to the 1979 and 1982–1993 models, pay attention to the stock fan. The 1979 models use a flex-blade fan. If you have one of these cars with the factory fan, check for cracks around the base of each blade.

In 1981, Ford replaced the flex-blade fan with a rigid plastic one, incorporating a clutch mechanism to engage and release the fan, depending on engine speed and temperature. In good shape, this clutch fan, in conjunction with the stock plastic shroud, works surprisingly well; yet, like the flex fan, it can suffer cracks over time. Furthermore, the clutch mechanism tends to wear out, causing slippage and allowing your Mustang to run hot, especially at idle.

Some people will step up and replace the stock fan with an electric one. Retrofitting the 1994-style fan to an older Mustang is the best bet for a street-going 5.0—this excellent fan is more than up to the job for cooling all but the most radically modified street machines. Not only will the electric fan help dissipate hot air inside the engine bay, but unlike a clutch fan, it won't rob the engine of additional power. It can also be switched off at speed to prevent airflow disruption, unlike the clutch fan, which turns whenever the engine is running.

When using an electric fan and a supercharger traditional electric fan mounted on the back of the radiator

Cracked or swollen hoses are defective and must be replaced. The thermostat can stick open or closed after a few years, and a buildup of scale will also compromise its abilities, so inspect and, if necessary, replace it. For most street SEFI cars, swapping out the stock 192-degree thermostat for a cooler one isn't recommended, unless you live in a hotter climate, like the southwest.

One of the most effective ways to improve cooling and engine efficiency on your 1982–1993 Mustang is to swap the stock clutch fan (which drains considerable power from the engine) for an electric one used on a 1994–1995 Mustang GT/Cobra, such as this one. A good source for these is Mustang Parts Specialties.

may interfere with the blower's serpentine belt drive, so you'll probably have to do some fiddling. Avoid dual electric fans, because they provide negligible cooling benefits over singles on street cars and can seldom be made to fit properly in conjunction with a supercharger.

Overheating problems can often be the result of the spring-loaded radiator pressure cap failing. If you've examined the rest of the cooling system and are replacing the radiator, as shown here, get the caap pressure tested—you might be surprised.

Water Pump

The stock water pump, often a source of cooling maladies on many vehicles, is surprisingly good on 5-liter Mustangs and seldom fails. However, if you have a hot rod engine under the hood and you're upgrading the rest of the cooling system, you might as well do the water pump too. High-performance pumps flow more coolant through the engine than the stock one, particularly at low rpm, which is great when your supercharged Mustang is stuck in traffic on a 100-degree day. Evans Cooling and FlowKooler are two good sources for replacement water pumps.

Oil Cooler

Fitted as standard on SSP and OPEC Mustangs, an oil-to-water cooler helped cool the oil passing through the bottom end of the 302 block.

If you live in a warmer climate and have a supercharged engine and/or an automatic transmission, consider purchasing an oil cooler.

Coolant

A top-quality cooling system is no good unless you use the right antifreeze. From the factory, 5-liter Mustangs used a 50/50 mix of ethylene-glycol-based coolant and water.

If you live in a northern climate, it's probably best to stick with the 50/50 mix for maximum protection.

If you live in a hotter climate and run a modified engine, there's no reason you can't go with a 70/30 water/coolant mix, topped with an additive such as Redline Water Wetter.

TRANSMISSION AND REAR END
Projects 19-21

PROJECT 19 ★ Replacing and Upgrading the Clutch Assembly

Time: 4 hours

Tools: Impact gun, adjustable torque wrench, sockets, screwdriver, clutch alignment tool, puller, slide hammer, soft hammer, lithium high-temperature grease

Talent: ★★★★

Applicable years: All stick-shift Mustangs

Parts: New clutch disc, pressure plate, new or remachined flywheel, new pilot bearing

Tab: $300

Tip: Properly machine your flywheel, either new or used, for better performance and shifting.

Performance Improvement: Improved shifting, performance, and driveline durability

One of the most common problems with stick-shift 5-liter Mustangs concerns the clutch. You'll come across hundreds of cars for sale in the *Trader* that say "need clutch work." Why? There are several reasons.

The first concerns the clutch itself. It was initially designed to work with a transmission that could handle a maximum of around 265 ft-lb of torque. Ford gradually improved matters, first by installing a self-adjusting mechanism in 1981 for reduced maintenance, along with a clutch/starter interlock (to prevent lurching the car when you turned the key). This was followed by enlarging the disc diameter from 10 to 10.5 inches in 1986, to cope with increased torque, and finally strengthening the transmission assembly in 1990, to match the engine's 300 ft-lb of torque output. Even so, the factory clutch is, by and large, barely adequate, even for a stock engine.

The second reason for failed clutches is abuse. Because many 5.0 owners are young and enthusiastic, they tend to drive their cars very hard—a burnout here, a five-grand clutch drop there, and, of course, power shifts. This generates tremendous heat and friction in the already weak clutch, causing the flywheel and disc to crack and warp and the pressure plate fingers to bend or break. Power-shifting strains the clutch cable, causing it to bind, fray, and even snap, and the plastic self-

adjusting quadrant often breaks. Is it any wonder that clutch replacement is one of those guarantees that seem to come with 5.0 ownership?

Installing a new clutch isn't too difficult a task, though you do need to bear a few things in mind. First, make sure you have a clutch alignment tool—refitting the transmission is almost impossible and very frustrating if

The factory hydraulic clutches installed in manual-transmission 5-liter Mustangs are barely adequate for a stock car and should be upgraded at the earliest opportunity, especially if you plan on modifying your Mustang. This stock clutch disc, pressure plate, and flywheel, removed from a 1988 GT, showed considerable wear. An upgraded assembly was just what the doctor ordered.

If your car is going to see mostly street duty with occasional excursions to the track, you don't want to install too heavy a clutch. For these applications, Ford Racing Performance Parts offers its King Cobra. Not surprisingly, it's an exact fit yet provides much greater clamping force while still retaining a fairly stock-style pedal feel. Note the size and number of the pressure springs, compared with those on the stocker.

the clutch disk isn't properly centered with the crankshaft. A puller for the pilot bushing is also quite handy.

It's tempting to install the strongest clutch you can find, but if your Mustang is mainly going to see street duty, the heavy pedal effort and chattering will make the car all but undrivable and will more likely than not increase wear on the transmission. Ideally you want a slightly overpowered clutch coupled to the transmission for maximum drivability and longevity.

Two of the most popular replacement clutches for street 5-liter Mustangs are the Ford Racing Performance Parts King Cobra and Centerforce's Dual Friction clutches. Like most aftermarket replacements, they offer a considerable increase in clamping force (up to 90 percent). However, the Centerforce clutches provide greater force without extra pedal effort, thanks to special weights mounted on the pressure-plate fingers. When the clutch pedal is up, the centrifugal force on these weights generates clamping force on the friction disk. Depressing the clutch pedal changes the weights' leverage angle, reducing their resistance to pedal effort. These weights take the place of heavy-duty clutch-plate springs in other products, allowing a stronger-than-stock clutch with a fairly light, stock pedal feel. As you begin to modify and coax more power at a greater rev range from your 5.0's engine, the Centerforce clutches are also good, because the greater the engine's rpm, the harder they grip.

To begin, make sure the car is securely supported on jack stands or a lift. Remove the H-pipe and driveshaft and unbolt the transmission. Also make sure that the engine is secured once the tranny has been dropped—using a hoist and supporting the motor from the top is a good idea, or if

When installing a new clutch, the flywheel must be clean. If your old one is in good shape, you can get it machined by a shop—alternatively, you can install a new one, as shown here.

you can't, use a jack to support it from underneath. In the latter case, be sure to use a piece of wood between the oil pan and the jack, to spread the weight of the engine across a greater area. You don't want to damage the oil pickup point, which is close to the bottom of the oil pan. If the pan gets damaged, it will affect oil circulation in the engine and may even result in engine seizure.

Remove the clutch slave cylinder, but keep the hydraulic line hooked up (otherwise you'll have to bleed the system). If you have a 1979 5.0 with the original-style mechanical clutch, remove the dust cover on the bell housing and disconnect the clutch cable and release lever. Then remove the bolts that secure the bell housing to the back of the engine and pull off the housing. It sometimes works to carefully pry off the alignment dowels with a flat-blade screwdriver.

At this point, it isn't really necessary to remove the clutch fork and release bearing from the bell housing; you can do this once all the clutch components are off the car. All you need to do is remove the bell housing from the tranny, followed by the clutch release lever from the ball stud. The bearing comes off the lever.

Once you've done this, grab your alignment tool and insert it into the center of the clutch-disc hub. Look for indexing marks on the pressure plate and flywheel. On a factory clutch, they're often marked with an X, O, or a white letter. If there aren't any, mark a spot on both the plate and flywheel so you can align them correctly when you put the clutch back together.

Start by loosening the bolts that secure the pressure plate to the flywheel by half a turn. Do this in a diagonal pattern, to release the spring pressure evenly. Remove the bolts and slowly pull out the pressure plate and clutch disc.

Remove the bolts that secure the flywheel to the crankshaft, making sure you firmly support the disc. Bear in mind

You'll need a special clutch alignment tool to center the clutch assembly. Push it all the way in, until it mates with the pilot bearing, then install the bolts. Tighten them in a diagonal pattern, to prevent uneven pressure. Once the alignment tool has been pulled out, tighten all the bolts to spec.

that stock 1979 cars used different-weight flywheels from 1982 and later ones, because the crankshafts were balanced differently. Pull the flywheel off and examine its condition, along with the pilot bearing, clutch disc, and pressure plate. If you see cracks, scoring, or heat blemishes on the flywheel and similar symptoms on the other components, or less than 1/8 inch of lining on the clutch plate, the clutch is extremely worn, and all components must be replaced.

The pilot bearing should be pulled for inspection and replacement—it's a good idea to install a new one when fitting a new clutch. To remove it, you need a special puller that attaches to a slide hammer (these can be sourced at most auto parts stores). Connect the puller to the pilot bearing and slowly pull the bearing out.

When installing a replacement clutch, consider whether to use a new flywheel or reuse your existing one. On most street 5.0s, where low-end torque is more of a factor, a steel flywheel will work more effectively and last longer. Aluminum flywheels, with their reduced inertia, are best reserved for high-horsepower drag and road-race cars, where the engine spends most of its operating range in a higher-rpm environment. If the flywheel is in good shape you can take it to a machine shop and have it resurfaced—a good idea if you're on a budget. It's also worthwhile getting this done on a new flywheel, just to make sure it's free of imperfections.

Before installing your new or machined flywheel, make sure that both it and the pressure plate are free of any oil,

grease, or other foreign objects. Attach the flywheel and install the new pilot bearing, first coating it in lithium grease. Push it into the recess with a soft hammer, making sure that the bearing seal faces outward, toward the tranny. Use the alignment tool to hold the new clutch disc and pressure plate in place, and make sure the clutch disc is installed the right way around (they're usually marked).

Install the pressure-plate-to-flywheel bolts, but only hand tighten them. Center the clutch disc by pushing the alignment tool in until it mates with the pilot bearing. Then you can begin tightening the pressure plate bolts some more. Do it gently and in a diagonal pattern, to prevent bending the pressure-plate cover. Torque the bolts to the required specs and pull out the alignment tool.

Lube the release bearing, lever, and contact patches with high-temperature grease. Reattach the bell housing to the transmission; torque all the bolts properly. Follow this by installing the tranny, clutch slave cylinder, self-adjusting cable (release cable on a 1979 Mustang), driveshaft, and finally the exhaust H-pipe. Make sure all bolts are correctly tightened.

Once you've installed your new clutch, take it easy for at least the first couple of weeks, to break it in (no power shifting, etc.)—otherwise you'll be back in the shop for another clutch before you know it.

Replacing the Self-Adjusting Mechanism

If you're upgrading the clutch on a 1982-and-up 5-liter, replace the cable and quadrant as well. Several companies, including Pro 5.0, Steeda, and Unlimited Performance, make replacement adjustable quadrants that are stronger than the stocker. They also allow you to tailor pedal engagement to your particular requirements to improve shifting and extend clutch life.

To replace the stock setup, disconnect the negative battery terminal (especially on airbag-equipped 1990-and-up Mustangs) and wait a few minutes before removing the steering wheel, column cover, and lower left part of the instrument panel, so you have clear and unobstructed access. Disconnect the master cylinder pushrod and brake light switch from the brake pedal. Now you should be able to access the plastic clutch quadrant and move it forward, until you can pull off the cable. Then slowly move the quadrant rearward, until it hits the stop.

Pull the cable forward through the firewall and disconnect the retainer that secures it to the T-5 bell housing. Remove all the electrical connectors on the steering column and pull the column from the brake pedal bracket. Unfasten the brake booster mounting nuts, to gain better access to the assembly. Now you can remove both the brake pedal support bracket (to which the self-adjusting quadrant is attached) and the clutch pedal. Once the support is free, pull the self-adjusting mechanism off the shaft that attaches to the bracket.

Chances are the plastic quadrant and pawl on the stocker will be scored and worn. When you install your replacement mechanism and clutch cable, keep the old springs and retaining fasteners, because you'll probably need at least one of them. Your replacement adjustable clutch quadrant will most likely come with an adjustable stop, which attaches to the top of the firewall, and a stronger, aluminum quadrant. Installing it is virtually the reverse of removing the stock assembly, keeping a few things in mind.

First, you'll probably need to add a spacer, to prevent the new quadrant from wobbling on its shaft once installed. When you've finally attached the adjuster to the firewall and the cable to the adjuster, play should be minimal when you press on the clutch pedal. This means that the quadrant is adjusted properly but that the cable can still move about 1/2 inch where it meets the clutch fork at the bottom.

With everything installed, the new quadrant and cable will complement your new clutch and make driving your 5-liter just that little bit easier, especially at slower speeds.

PROJECT 20 ★

Beefing Up the Automatic Transmission

Time: 52 hours

Tools: Professional transmission builder and shop

Talent: ★★★★

Applicable years: 1986–1995

Parts: Torque converter, input shaft, transmission cooler, servo, overdrive bands, valve body improvement kit, clutches, filter

Tab: $1,500–$4,000

Tip: Seek a good transmission builder who understands your needs.

Performance Improvement: Improved performance and durability while maintaining pleasant street manners and fuel economy

Complementary Project: Rear-end gears and cooling system upgrade

If you own a factory stock 5-liter Mustang with an automatic transmission, you're at somewhat of a disadvantage, especially when it comes to cars equipped with the AOD, essentially Ford's veteran C4 with an overdrive gear. From 1984, when this transmission was introduced on V-8 Mustangs, through 1985, it was teamed exclusively with the central fuel-injected 302 V-8, which was around 10 (later 30) horses shy of its carbureted equivalent and was ill suited to serious performance modification.

Things improved from 1986, when the fuel-injected V-8 was available either with the AOD or the five-speed manual gearbox. Automatics use more energy than manual gearboxes, from lack of a direct union between the engine and transmission. Even the 1987 AOD-equipped 5-liter Mustangs still had a 5-horsepower disadvantage compared to their stick-shift brethren.

The AOD also poses a problem because it has very gentle shift calibrations from Ford and a weak two-piece input shaft that locks up third gear at cruising speeds, to boost fuel economy—qualities not ideally suited to a high-torque muscle car. Combined with a substantially hot-rodded 302 motor, the result is often toast. Blown overdrive bands, broken shafts, and worn clutches are common, so if you're planning on upgrading your engine and wish to keep your AOD, consider strengthening it. Mustangs have different needs, and you have to know what your goal is with the car. Even strengthened or "built" racing automatic transmissions are not alike.

Although a transmission upgrade/rebuild is beyond the scope of this book, it's still a good idea to find out how to strengthen your AOD to handle greater-than-stock power and torque.

Primary things to consider when upgrading your AOD: Torque Converter

The right torque converter is crucial to any performance automatic transmission buildup. It has an input shaft going through it to the engine and consists of three parts: the impeller, bolted to the back of the flywheel, the turbine, and stator. The converter's job is similar to a clutch in stick-shift cars, except that it works by fluid

Most 5-liter Mustangs that shift gears themselves are equipped with this—Ford's automatic overdrive (AOD) transmission. Although the stock version is less than ideal for performance applications and has a reputation for breakage, you can do a number of things to strengthen and improve it.

Choosing the right torque converter is crucial to maximizing performance and longevity from your slushbox. You need to take into account the power and torque of your engine, rear-end axle ratios, and other factors.

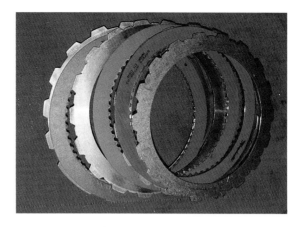

When considering an automatic transmission upgrade, another area you must pay attention to concerns the stock clutches. They are too small and too few (five) in number to cope effectively with aggressive shift calibrations and modified engine shift calibrations and modified engine and often contribute to slippage and heat buildup, especially when the tranny shifts into third gear. Consider replacing them with heavyduty aftermarket items.

coupling between the impeller and turbine. The stator redirects transmission fluid from the turbine back to the impeller, which multiplies the force of fluid entering the impeller and thus torque as well. Besides creating energy, the transmission fluid flows through passages inside the tranny, which, via clutch packs, controls shift points.

Changing the converter has a direct effect on stall speed (the biting point at which the transmission engages the wheels) and the Mustang's overall performance characteristics. As a general rule, smaller-diameter converters are good for highly modified engines, because their reduced rotating mass generates less energy. That quality, along with wider-spaced fins on the casing, bumps up the stall speed, bringing the AOD's shifting range in line with modified engines that operate well above the agricultural-like stock power band.

When selecting a converter, you really need to work with an experienced Mustang/transmission shop. Selecting the right one depends on many factors, such as engine cam specs, torque output, rear-end gears, and other internal modifications to your AOD, such as the type of input shaft, transmission ratios, and shift kit. There are plenty of stories where a couple of individuals whose Mustangs were similar in performance went with the same converter—one ran great, the other ran terrible. (Another advantage of working with a shop is that if something goes wrong, you'll have someone to take up the issue with. If a reputable shop produces an unsatisfactory result, they should make it right.)

Input Shaft

Attaching to the crank and passing through the center of the converter is the input shaft. From the factory, the AOD found in 1984–1993 5-liter Mustangs has a two-piece steel lockup input shaft (later cars have a three-piece unit). Although it's great for smooth shifting and fuel economy,

once you start playing around, especially if you install a valve-body improvement kit, the firmer shifting that results puts tremendous strain on the stock shaft—particular during the second-to-third upshift, where it locks up third gear once the Mustang reaches cruising velocity. Without this lockup, the slow-turning torque converter would generate too much slippage, friction, and heat. The increased strain will eventually cause the shaft to break.

Therefore, if you're thinking of installing such a kit, consider replacing the shaft with a stronger aftermarket piece, such as the billet lockups available from Precision Industries. The billet construction provides a notable increase in strength over the stocker, while still retaining lockup—essential for fuel economy. Non-lockup one-piece units are best reserved for drag cars, where maximum durability and torque multiplication are the name of the game, and fuel economy doesn't even factor in.

Valve-Body Improvement Kit

Commonly referred to as a "shift kit"—though this term is actually owned by TransGo, who have long been in the automatic transmission improvement business—a valve-body improvement kit firms up the stock shift patterns, usually by boosting line pressure or rerouting the automatic transmission fluid path. Some even allow you to customize shift patterns to suit a particular driver's needs. With the lazy shift calibrations from Ford, installing such a kit should be one of your priorities, even on an almost bone-stock automatic Mustang.

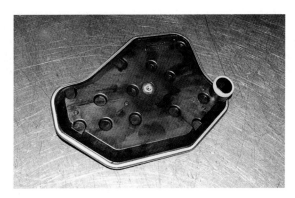

A high-performance filter is often overlooked when it comes to automatic transmissions. Replacing the stock filter with a free-flowing item will reduce clogging, friction, and fluid leakage.

Popular vendors for these kits for 5-liter Mustangs include Baumann Engineering, Level 10, and TransGo. The latter's shift kits are recommended on AODs, since TransGo, unlike many kits, reroutes the shift path rather than boosting line pressure. Boosted line pressure can cause friction, heat buildup, and premature internal wear on an already fairly fragile stock gearbox.

If you own a 1994–1995 Mustang with the AOD-E (electronic) version, you have a few additional things to consider. Baumann's valve-body improvement kits are especially worth considering, because the AOD-E uses a piggyback system, in which the EEC-IV governs and supplements the hydraulics to control the transmission's operation and shift patterns. If you start modifying your engine or install steeper gearing without paying attention to the EEC-IV, the computer can't compensate for the changes, and you'll end up with a car that's awkward to drive, with mismatched shift points and internal transmission problems.

Baumann's kit for these applications, the Baumannator, wires up to the stock harness and is particularly effective. It allows you to tune and custom-adjust shift points and to control torque converter operation via a laptop and Windows-compatible software, to match your driveline combination. Alternatively, veteran transmission shop Level 10 is extremely experienced in AOD-Es and can recalibrate your stock slushbox to suit your 1994–1995 5-liter's particular engine and gearing setup, as well as your own driving style.

Servo
On stock 5-liters, the factory B-servo can eventually cause slippage and wear on the overdrive bands as the tranny shifts from third gear into overdrive, especially if your engine has received upgrades. Swapping the stock servo for an A-servo as found in the supercharged 1989–1997 Ford Thunderbird/Mercury Cougar, with its

increased clamping force on the overdrive bands, is a great way to reduce slippage and improve durability.

Overdrive Bands
The factory bands on the stock AOD are small and tend to slip, wear, and break during extended hard driving—especially in third and fourth gears. Consider swapping them for stouter ones. A low-buck way is to install the bigger, 2-inch-diameter bands found in 1994–1995 AOD-Es. Other transmission parts suppliers, such as Precision Industries, also offer quality replacement bands designed to handle high-horsepower engine loads and firm shifts.

Clutches
The clutch discs in the stock clutch pack are too few and too weak to harness energy effectively on a modified 5-liter. Consequently, they often wear out. Stepping up to stronger aftermarket clutch packs is therefore something to consider. Recommended vendors for replacement clutch packs include Alto and Kolene, but discuss the matter with a specialist Mustang/Transmission shop for the best advice for your situation.

Transmission Filter
If you've ever looked underneath an AOD-equipped Mustang that has received bolt-on modifications and seen automatic tranny fluid dripping out, it may be a result of a clogged stock filter. The filter is restrictive at the best of times, but if it's old, it can really clog the flow of fluid, causing it to seek another path—often between the valve body separator plates. Leaking is especially problematic on a high-horsepower 5-liter, where the fluid is heated up even more and greater friction results inside the transmission. Replacing the stocker with a less restrictive aftermarket filter, such as those available from Precision Industries, is therefore a wise investment.

Cooler
Heat is perhaps the AOD's worst enemy. It causes fluid breakdown, which results in friction and eventually leads to wear of the transmission's internals and even seizure. Even if you have a stock automatic 5-liter, a cooler can make your transmission's life easier and longer, especially if you drive the car frequently. The cooler can be plumbed into the factory cooling tube and will help significantly reduce the temperature of the fluid. It will also take some of the strain off the factory cooling system, which uses part of the main radiator as a transmission cooler. On a modified 5-liter, the more power you make, the more heat you generate—thus a top-notch tranny cooler becomes crucial in transmission longevity.

PROJECT 21 ★ Installing Steeper Rear-End Gears

Time: 4 hours

Tools: Impact gun, adjustable torque wrench, sockets, screwdriver, lithium high-temperature grease, special Ford service tool, dial indicator, shims

Talent: ★★★★

Applicable years: 1986–1995

Parts: New ring and pinion, clutches, gear oil, differential

Tab: $350

Tip: Unless you're really experienced, leave this job to a pro.

Performance Improvement: Improved torque multiplication and acceleration

During the 5-liter Mustang's long production run, two styles of rear end were employed. In the early days (1979–1985), Ford mated its trusty 7.5-inch solid axle to the rear control arms. Given that the 1979 302 couldn't muster more than 240 ft-lb of torque in stock form, and even the 1983–1985 four-barrel engines made only 245 to 270 ft-lb, this fairly small rear was perfectly adequate. To provide better offline bite, Ford offered 3.08, 3.27, and even 3.45:1 axle ratios (yes, on manual transmissions) and, thankfully, from 1981 a Traction-Lok limited differential. This uses internal gear friction to direct more torque to the rear wheel with the most traction, reducing wheelspin and increasing off-the-line bite (just ask anybody who's driven a powerful V-8, rear-drive car with an open diff, particularly in the wet).

For 1986, when Ford switched the 5-liter Mustang to sequential fuel injection, among the parts to be upgraded was the rear end. In place of the old 7.5, FoMoCo substituted the 8.8, also found on its Ranger compact pickup truck. This was distinguished externally by a differential cover that was flat on all sides, whereas the 7.5 was flat only on the top and bottom. The new rear was more than 30 percent stronger than its predecessor, but alas, the final drive ratios were dropped—2.73 and optional 3.08:1 for five-speed cars. Automatics, in part to compensate for the gentle tranny shift calibrations and greater parasitic power loss, got steeper 3.08:1 as standard, with 3.27:1 optional. You can tell what factory gears your Mustang has by looking at the data tag on the driver's door. M identifies 2.73, while Z and E are for 3.08 and 3.27:1, respectively.

The tall 2.73:1 axle ratio found in the majority of stock 5-speed 302 Mustangs is a major Achilles' heel for lightning-quick takeoffs. Just replacing it with steeper axle ratios can make a huge difference in acceleration. However, the 2.73 was chosen largely on the basis of fuel economy and fast highway driving, particularly for law enforcement agencies, which snapped up thousands of 5-liter Fox Mustang coupes in the 1980s and early 1990s.

When considering a gear swap, the general rule is that the higher the numerical ratio, the greater the acceleration but the lower the top speed. More gear is nice, but you need to match it to your engine's operating range and the transmission's gear ratios. While some people say that the shorter the ratio the better, too much can be

Swapping your stock final-drive ratios for a steeper replacement ring and pinion, such as this one from Precision Gear, is one of the best bang-for-the-buck projects you can do on your 5-liter Mustang.

a pain, especially on a street car. Gearing that's too low causes premature wear on the engine and other driveline components, not to mention making your Mustang a chore to drive, particularly on the highway—no one wants to be cruising at 65 mph with the engine turning at 5,000 rpm.

The aftermarket, including companies like Ford Racing Performance Parts, Precision Gear, Pro 5.0, and Richmond, offers a huge selection of axle ratios—the most common being 3.27, 3.55, 3.73, 4.10, 4.30, and 4.56 through 4.88, and even 5.13:1. For most street-going 5.0s, especially those using essentially stock engines and stock transmission ratios, consider going with a set of 3.55 gears in five-speed cars and 3.73 for automatics, to get the most bang for your buck. This will usually provide the best

When you pull off the stock differential cover, this is probably what you'll see—the Traction-Lok differential. Because you'll be pulling out the ring and pinion for a gear swap, this is also a good time to check the condition of your Traction-Lok and replace it if necessary.

balance between acceleration, drivability, reliability, and fuel economy. If you plan on going road racing, where higher speeds and aerodynamics are more important than off-the-line grunt, you'll probably want to select ratios between 3.27 and 3.55, because many classes permit limited engine modifications as well.

Many street enthusiasts will step up to 3.73 on stick applications and 4.10 for automatics, but these increase the risk of breakage and are best suited to cars that spend a considerable amount of time at the drag strip, where torque multiplication and quick acceleration are the name of the game, top speed be damned. They're also best suited to cars using power adders or seriously modified high-revving engines, because these steeper ratios can more effectively exploit the engine's power. Many 5-liter pilots have destroyed a sizable number of transmissions (particularly AODs) by putting 4.10 gears in essentially stock Mustangs.

Anything above 4.10 is best left to quarter-mile thrashers. However, if you install a T56 six-speed transmission, you can still technically run 4.10s or 4.88s on the street, though engine longevity on most pushrod 302s and gas mileage will be questionable at best.

Although a rear-end gear swap represents tremendous performance per dollar, especially compared to other mods, it's quite tricky to do right and is best left to a professional shop mechanic who has considerable expe-

rience working on rear ends and all the proper tools. Even so, it's worth watching, because it will give you an insight into what goes into this process.

What a Rear Gear Swap Entails

To begin with, a special press is required for installing the bearing on the pinion gear. You'll also need to check the depth of the pinion, using a special Ford service tool for rear ends. If it's not in spec, the pinion will need to be shimmed until it is. Once installed, the pinion will require proper torquing to set preload. Also, clearance between the ring gear and pinion must be precise and should be checked with a dial indicator and adjusted with shims. The clearance, known as backlash, is generally set loose to achieve quiet, smooth gears. Unskillful gear installations will often result in considerable rear-end axle whine and premature wear, in part from to too tight a backlash between ring teeth and pinion.

Another thing that goes hand in hand with a gear swap is recalibrating the speedometer gears in the transmission, which requires removing the tranny from the car. The factory plastic speedo gears on five-speed cars can wear out quickly (if your speedometer needle bounces up and down, the gear is probably on its way out). Not only that, correct speedo calibration also requires considerable math, for although Ford supplies

Many things need to be addressed when doing a rear gear swap, including making sure your speedometer is properly calibrated with the change in final drive ratio. Ford supplies replacement plastic speedo gears, though you need to make sure you select the right ones to correspond with your new rear gears.

When upgrading the rear-end gears, pay special attention to the differential and the axles. Over time, especially if the Mustang is subjected to numerous hard drag launches, the differential clutches can wear out, causing it to slip. If your 5-liter has a generous number of miles under its belt, it would be worth inspecting the Traction-Lok when doing the gears. If you want to replace it, the Auburn High Torque and Torsen Traction-Lok differentials are good, slightly more durable substitutes and support both the factory 28-spline and bigger 31-spline axles.

Speaking of the stock axles, the factory 28-spliners work okay on a stock 5-liter but become susceptible to breakage once you start putting significantly more power to the ground. (Go to a drag racing event and chances are you'll see a street-driven Mustang break one of

replacement speedo gears, you need to work out which one is compatible with your new rear-end ratio.

The speedo gears are housed inside the transmission. Although they're not too tricky to access on stick-shift 5-liters, getting at them requires pulling off the tranny tail shaft. On automatic Mustangs, the drive gears are integrated and machined with the tranny output shaft, so the whole transmission has to be pulled apart to replace them. From this, you can see that a gear swap is not for the fainthearted.

The stock 8.8 rear (you shouldn't use a 7.5 with a modified engine) found in most 5-liter Mustangs isn't bad. From the factory it had 28-spline axles with either four or five (1993 Cobra and 1994–1995 Mustangs) lugs, held in place by C-clips and turned by the fairly reliable Traction-Lok differential. The differential itself works by pushing side gears and uses layers of clutch packs to engage and turn the axles. When pulled out of the axle housing, the stock Traction-Lok can be identified by the S-shaped spring in the middle section.

them.) A cost-effective way to remedy this problem is to install the stouter 31-spline axles from Ford Racing Performance Parts that originally came in Ford trucks.

If you're shooting for the low 12-second zone at the drag strip, you'll have to eschew stock axles, because the C-clips that hold them in place can fail, causing the axles to work their way loose—not something you want while racing down the strip. The most popular solution for drag cars is stronger axles that work with C-clip eliminators, such as those available from Moser. These eliminators feature bearings mounted inside an aluminum case to keep the axles in check, though for regular high-power street cars and road racing, consider stepping up to stronger 9-inch bearings, which can handle both straight line and side loading (the others can handle only drag launches).

Companies like Currie Enterprises, Strange Engineering (and, of course, Moser) are experts in the field of rear ends and will steer you in the right direction when you're looking to upgrade your solid axle.

PROJECT 22 ★ *Installing Subframe Connectors*

Time: 2 hours

Tools: MIG welder, sander, drill, torque wrench, sockets, Sharpie marker

Talent: ★★★

Applicable years: All

Tab: $80–$150

Parts: Subframe connectors, bolts

Tip: When doing this project, make sure the Mustang is supported by its own suspension, such as by a drive-on ramp that can be raised.

Performance Improvement: Much-needed chassis strengthening, improved overall performance and agility

One of the biggest problems concerning the 5-liter Mustang, especially the 1979–1993 version, is the inherent lack of body stiffness.

When a succession of more powerful 302s found their way beneath the hood in the mid-1980s, problems began to surface. The V-8 cars received little in the way of extra frame bracing. The combination of the 5.0 engine, overly enthusiastic driving by many owners, and the flimsy Fox chassis—particularly the lack of a true backbone or connection between the front and rear frame-rail assemblies—soon caused many of these Mustangs to loosen up and flex. This causes the suspension attachment points to move and, at worst, produces structural cracks around the torque boxes, rockers, inner fenders, and C-pillars.

The lack of structural stiffness was so bad that Ford paid great attention to correcting it when they redesigned the Mustang for 1994. Increased curb weight and elimination of the hatchback body style were a direct result of these efforts.

Fortunately for the Fox enthusiast, help is at hand, in the shape of subframe connectors. Although this project concerns primarily the original Fox cars, even the 1994–1995 5-liters can benefit from further stiffening. As their name implies, subframe connectors are pieces of steel or chrome moly that link the front and rear sheetmetal-formed frame rails, effectively adding a backbone to the chassis on each side. Subframe connectors are widely available through the aftermarket and come in two forms—bolt-on and pure weld-in.

Bolt-on connectors usually have integral brackets at both ends that fit over the stock frame rails, with

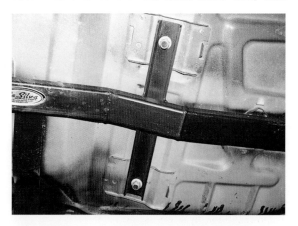

One the first projects you should consider for any 5-liter Mustang (especially the Fox version) is a set of subframe connectors, to reduce body flex. Many styles are available, although pieces that incorporate crossbracing reinforcement for the seat mounting holes, such as this one, are among the best.

Subframe connectors do exactly as the name suggests, joining the front and rear frame rails to form a true backbone. Put the car on a ramp, so it's still supporting its own weight, and weld your connectors, even if they come supplied with bolts and integral brackets, as here.

Besides providing chassis stiffening, subframe connectors make great jacking points, because they're strong enough to support the weight. Shown is an old-style connector that's simply a piece of square steel tubing, cut and welded in. These basic pieces are still effective and are a good idea if you're really on a budget.

mounting holes for the bolts. They offer a slightly easier installation, particularly when it comes to aligning the connectors with the factory frame rails, though you'll need to drill bolt holes in the rails. Even the bolt-on connectors then must be welded in place, to add stiffness. If not welded, these connectors still allow motion when subjected to cornering forces. Bolting them is primarily to secure them in the correct position before you weld them permanently in place.

Weld-in connectors come in many shapes and forms. Some are simply crude, rectangular steel bars welded between the frame rails; others are more elaborate affairs that mate exactly with the contours of the stock front- and rear-frame rails. Some include extra bracing for the torque boxes and floorpans, while still others are part of a complete chassis upgrade kit. If your Mustang is going to be limited to mostly street use, with the occasional drag strip excursion, a pair of simple weld-on connectors will be more than adequate; they should be made from good-quality, heavy-gauge steel for maximum effectiveness.

If your aspirations lean more toward greater drag-strip or road-course driving, consider a complete chassis upgrade package complete with connectors, torque arms, mounting bolts, strut tower, and g-load braces.

When it comes to installing subframe connectors, take your car to a shop or perform the task with experienced help or supervision. You'll need to put the car on a ramp and make sure the wheels and suspension are supporting its weight while you install the connectors. Otherwise, if you lift the wheels in the air, the chassis will flex, and you won't be able to install the connectors properly. You should also have access to good-quality welding apparatus (a MIG welder is recommended) and proper safety equipment.

Before installing the connectors, test fit them one at a time, to make sure they fit properly. If so, the next step is to mark where they'll be welded. Scrape away material (including, paint, undercoating, or even rust) around each area to be welded, until it's down to the bare metal. This will help the weld penetrate and bond the metal better, resulting in a stronger and more secure weld. Once you've done this, you can begin welding in the connectors one at a time. Having an extra pair of hands is extremely helpful—nothing is worse than having to redo welds on misaligned connectors.

Most aftermarket subframe connectors will require welding only at the front and rear attachments, where they meet the factory frame rails. Some, such as the Steeda Double Cross and Kenny Brown pieces, feature crossbraces that attach to the seat mounting attachments in the floorpan for greater stiffness. (If you're using these, lift the interior carpet to prevent damaging it from underneath while welding.) Still others, such as those from Maximum Motorsports, require welding both ends and the center portion of the subframe connector to the body.

Once the connectors have been installed and the welds have set, paint or powder coat the connectors and their attachment points. When you're done, carefully lower the car back onto terra firma.

PROJECT 23 ★ Installing a Strut Tower and g-Load Brace

Time: 2 hours

Tools: Impact gun, adjustable torque wrench, sockets, drill, Sharpie marker, portable MIG welder

Talent: ★★

Applicable years: All

Tab: $80–$150

Parts: Strut tower brace, g-load brace, bolts and fasteners

Tip: Pinch-weld your strut brace at the firewall for best results.

Performance Improvement: Increased chassis strength, better handling, steering response, agility

Not as fundamental for chassis stiffness as subframe connectors but still an important piece in the unibody strengthening puzzle are strut tower and g-load braces. These two items become particularly important if you plan on serious corner carving in your 5-liter, but even on street cars (particularly the 1979–1993 variety), they're worth considering, because they'll help tie the unibody down and make your Mustang handle better in the turns.

Strut Tower Brace

If you own a Fox-body car, the best way to start is with the strut tower brace. On the SN95 cars, Ford has already done half the chassis stiffening for you—among other things, these cars came from the factory with strut braces. Therefore, unless you're planning to build a serious road-race handler from your 1994 or 1995 V-8 Mustang, you don't really need to replace your stock strut brace with an aftermarket one.

The purpose of the strut tower brace is to reduce torsional chassis flex, which it does by joining the shock towers and the firewall. Combined with subframe connectors, the brace will make a noticeable difference in the overall stiffness and driving characteristics of your older Fox 5-liter, especially those convertibles, which have considerable cowl shake from the factory. However, as with many other upgrades for the 5.0, not all strut braces are created equal. When looking to install one, it should have two or more attachment points to the shock towers on each side and preferably be triangular or trapezoidal, with sizable area where it attaches to the firewall. The larger and more numerous the attachment points, the stiffer the result. Companies such as Eibach, HPM, MAC, Steeda, Saleen, and Jamex all offer good-quality strut tower braces, with the Steeda pieces in particular being popular.

Installing a strut brace is relatively straightforward—it simply bolts up to the shock tower and firewall. Also get a backing plate that attaches between the brace and the firewall, to further increase stiffness (some strut braces, such as HPM's, come with these).

Before you begin the installation, test fit the brace and backing plate. If your Mustang already has a modified engine with a bigger and taller aftermarket intake, you may face clearance problems with a prefab brace. In this case, it might be best to fabricate your own, in conjunction with an experienced Mustang shop.

If you like going around corners in your Fox Mustang, installing a strut tower brace is a great idea. It will help stiffen the flimsy unibody. Many types of strut braces are available, including chrome ones to complement dressed-up engine bays. Most come supplied with bolts and fittings.

Shown here is a strut brace installed on a 1992 Mustang GT. Even if you drive your car only on the street, the difference in stiffness and handling is quite noticeable. The owner of this car drives it every day and takes it road racing once in a while. *Evan Smith*

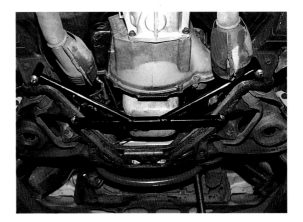

Along with a strut brace, installing a chassis steering brace or g-load brace (as it's often referred to in Mustang circles) will help, because it prevents the frame rails from flexing and keeps your car pointed in the direction you want to go. This brace has angled arms in addition to the tubular crossmember, for greater stiffness and improved steering precision. *Evan Smith*

If all appears well up to this point, have a colleague hold the brace in position while you mark the attachment points. Next, where you've marked, carefully drill holes for the strut mounting bolts on the firewall and each of the front strut towers. Make sure when you're done that they correspond in size to the bolts themselves. The best way to get an exact result is to trace around the inside of the bolt hole in the brace, set the brace aside, then strike directly in the center of the circle with a punch. This will make an impression to guide your drill bit.

Start with a bit that's smaller than you need and work up gradually to one that's the same diameter as the mounting bolt. Doing it this way allows you several opportunities to check that the hole you're making is dead center on your mark. If it isn't, when you change to the next bigger bit, point it slightly in the direction you need to go to get it back to center.

Most prefab strut braces include all mounting hardware, so in most cases it's simply a matter of securing the brace and accompanying bolts in place and torquing them to the recommended specifications. It's also a good idea to pinch-weld the attachments at the firewall, to maximize the brace's stiffening ability.

g-Load Brace

A g-load brace, while not as fundamentally important as frame connectors or a strut brace, can still contribute significantly to overall chassis stiffness. In fact, some companies, such as Eibach, often sell this and the strut tower brace together, for maximum effectiveness. Saleen Motorsports coined the term g-load for its own chassis steering brace, though several manufacturers offer comparable products. These braces work by bolting to the two front frame rails, thus reducing the tendency for the rails to deflect inward under hard cornering or braking. They improve steering precision and aid front-end alignment (particularly on the 1979–1993 Mustangs).

These chassis braces fall primarily into two categories: basic metal tubes with twin attachment points at each end, or more complex pieces with angled arms that link up to your Mustang's frame in four locations instead of two. The latter provide bracing over a greater area and are thus more effective.

Installing these will, like the strut brace, be a bolt-on affair, requiring you to drill holes at the attachment points. Therefore, you'll need to test fit the brace and mark the holes correctly before installation, to prevent poor alignment. Because you'll be working underneath the car, you'll need to put it on a lift or support it on axle stands and remove the front wheels. This will provide much easier access and flexibility when installing the g-load or chassis steering brace. Check fit and alignment of the brace first, then carefully drill the holes for the brace bolts. Make sure you tighten all the fittings correctly. Once you're done, reinstall the two front wheels and carefully lower the car.

PROJECT 24 ★ *Upgrading the Front Brakes*

Time: 6 hours

Tools: Impact gun, adjustable torque wrench, sockets, Torx socket, screwdriver, pickle fork, air chisel, double-flare tool kit, grinding wheel, threaded press

Talent: ★★★★

Applicable years: 1979–1993

Tab: $650

Parts: New master cylinder, bigger calipers, pads, brake line fittings, replacement front rotors, brake lines, fittings

Tip: Flare your brake line fittings before you begin, to save time.

Performance Improvement: Improved safety and stopping power

One of the cheapest and most cost-effective ways to improve stopping ability on your Fox 5-liter is to invest in a replacement front brake package. The stock discs and 60 mm single-piston calipers, even on the 1987–1993 cars, are woefully inadequate for a 3,200-pound car that can run 14-second ETs right out of the box. Considering that the front end bears the brunt of braking friction, upgrading your front rotors, calipers, and pads can make a sizable difference.

One approach that retains the Fox Mustang's four-lug bolt pattern is to install 11-inch late-model rotors (if you own a 1979 or 1982–1986 5-liter that came with wimpy 10.06 in units), along with bigger calipers. Kenny Brown's Club Sport package is a particularly good value. This kit (designed to work with 1987–1993 Mustangs) includes stronger, steel 73 mm piston calipers and a bigger master cylinder (derived from those used on the Lincoln Mark VII), along with an adjustable proportioning valve and performance pads. Although the kit consists mainly of parts-bin stuff, it provides a better-quality, safer alternative to true junkyard pieces. By combining the kit with the 11-inch-diameter rotors, you still have enough clearance to retain the factory 15- or 16-inch wheels—also essential for the budget minded.

First, block the rear wheels and apply the parking brake. Then jack up the car, support it on axle stands or a lift, and remove the front wheels. Work on one side at a time, to keep things straight. With the rim off, next is

Will you look at this! Zero to 60 mph in 6 seconds, and 60 mph back to 0 in two weeks, thanks to these puny calipers and small 10.8-inch discs. To say the stock brakes on Fox 5-liter Mustangs (such as this 1988 LX) are barely adequate is like saying mice like cheese. Unless you plan on preserving your car in its as-delivered state, consider a brake upgrade mandatory.

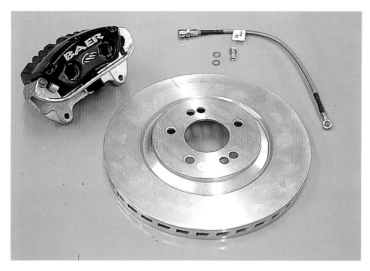

One of the most popular front brake upgrade kits is the Club Sport package from Kenny Brown, though other vendors, such as Ford Racing Performance Parts, are also great sources for upgrading the weak factory anchors. If your budget is a little less stringent, Baer provides brake upgrades for 5-liter Mustangs that work with both four- and five-lug wheels, though you'll probably need to upgrade to 17-inch wheels. *Evan Smith*

With the caliper unbolted and pushed aside, remove the outer bearings and pull off the old discs.

the caliper hose. Early Fox Mustangs hoses screw directly into the caliper, while 1987–1993 5-liter cars have banjo-style fittings. On the latter, remove the union bolt and the sealing washers. Wrap the end of the hose in a sealed plastic bag, to prevent fluid leakage or contamination.

Use a Torx socket to remove the slider bolts that secure the caliper, and slowly pull it off. Remove the stock rotors. (If your front rotors are badly scored and need machining or replacing, this is a good time to do it.) To remove the rotors, take off the dust cap in the center with a flat-blade screwdriver and remove the cotter pin that secures the wheel-bearing retaining nut. Then you can simply pull the rotor off.

If you own a 1986 or earlier 5-liter, you'll also need to change to 1987-and-up rotors to use the Kenny Brown kit. You'll also need to change the front spindles on these cars, because the 1987-and-up rotors must be mounted on 1987-and-up spindles. (If you remove the spindles, also remove the bolts that secure them to the struts, and support the lower control arm with a jack to prevent the spring from popping out.)

Remove the ball joint nut and use a pickle-fork attachment on an air chisel (recommended) or a hammer and pickle fork to remove the spindle from the ball joint. If you're going through this process, replace any worn ball joints and bushings.

Next, install 11-inch diameter rotors. If your car came with these and they're in good shape, you can reuse them. Machining them on a lathe is a good idea, especially if they've been on the Mustang for a while. This is also a good time to install new wheel bearings and seals and to repack the front hubs with grease.

With the rotors back on the Mustang, we can now install our new calipers. If you're using the Kenny Brown pieces, they'll slot in place of the stockers on 1987–1993 cars. If you have an older Fox Mustang, you'll need different slider bolts (available through Ford) to mount these calipers.

Next up are the performance brake pads. The pads used in the Kenny Brown kit are the same size as the OEM pads but use a different anti-rattle clip to fit the Kenny Brown calipers. If you have OEM style pads you will need to modify them in order to fit the Lincoln style calipers, often by removing the anti-rattle clip.

Braided stainless-steel brake lines can be used with any front brake upgrade. These are recommended,

If you're performing a front brake upgrade on a 1986-or-earlier Fox Mustang, you'll often need to change the front spindles too, because the 1987–1993 pieces that most front brakes are designed to work with are of a slightly different design. Support the lower control arm when doing this, to prevent the spring from popping out.

because they're more durable and don't expand under high pressure, like the stockers. On 1987-and-up Mustangs, they fit in place of the factory pieces, but on earlier cars with screw-in line fittings, you'll need to obtain a set of banjo-style fitting bolts (also available via Ford). Secure the lines to the brake brackets on the inside of the fenders as well.

With a brake upgrade such as the Club Sport package, you'll need to do a number of brake-line nut swaps. Therefore, the brake lines will need to be cut to remove and replace the original fittings. A good way to do this and to make sure you won't suffer from brake failure and will pass state or provincial safety inspection is to use a double-flare tool kit.

Although you can do this at home, it's a good idea to work with a qualified technician. Cut off the old flare, to remove the original line nut, and use a tubing cutter to make a straight, burr-free cut. Use a sharp wheel below the flare and tighten it until it's snug. Rotate and tighten the wheel around the brake line until the flare is cut free.

Place the line into a clamp, making sure the wing nuts are tight. Mark the die used to make the initial flare, so you can see how much line should be exposed between the clamp and the flare. Insert the correct die into the end of the brake line and attach a threaded press to it, tightening it until it bottoms out. Then loosen it. Remove the die and retighten the press into the end of the line. Voilà! You now have a double flare, which is essential on brake lines—single flares, such as those on fuel lines, are not adequate for brakes.

Next up on the brake upgrade is the new master cylinder and properly plumbing the brake system. First, remove the old master cylinder. They can be categorized into two types: 1979–1986 and 1987–1993. The former used a cast-iron cylinder, whereas the latter used an aluminum cylinder with a transparent plastic brake reservoir. On 1979–1986 cars, only the front line nut must be changed. On 1987–1993 cars, install new fittings for both master cylinder lines. On 1987-and-up Mustangs, the bottom line going into the master cylinder must also be rerouted to a kit-supplied T-fitting, but older cars already have the necessary routing in place with the stock master cylinder.

Next up is the adjustable proportioning valve. Unscrew the lines from the brass junction by the right hood hinge and replace the junction with the adjustable proportioning valve, incorporating the brass adapters that come with the kit. The new valve determines the amount of pressure the rear brakes require, so remove the plunger from the stock proportioning valve, because you no longer need it. Leave the proportioning valve wide open and bleed the brakes, then decrease rear line pressure by one full turn. This should result in the front brakes locking before the rears under hard stops while keeping your Mustang in a straight line upon deceleration.

BRAKES

PROJECT 25 ★ *Performing a Four-Wheel Disc Brake and Five-Lug Conversion*

Time: 18 hours

Tools: Impact gun, wrenches, adjustable torque wrench, sockets, screwdriver, ball-peen hammer, rubber hose, clear container, jack, axle stands, tube cutter, double-flare tool kit, grinding wheel, keen assistant

Talent: ★★★★

Applicable years: 1979–1993 (except SVT Cobra)

Tab: $850

Parts: Spindles, dust shields, struts, axles, calipers, brake pads, rotors, brake cables, mounting brackets, required bolts and fittings

Tip: Buy a complete five-lug package from a quality Mustang salvage yard—it will save you time and frustration.

Performance Improvement: Improved stopping power and handling, greater versatility when upgrading brakes, wheels, and tires

One of the most popular modifications on Fox 5-liter Mustangs is the so-called five-lug conversion. Along with inadequate brakes, Ford decided to install four-lug-bolt wheels on all regular production Mustangs through 1993. This poses a few obstacles for enthusiasts upgrading to larger brakes and selecting aftermarket wheels and tires, the majority of which are designed to work with five-lug rotors and axles. Furthermore, major brake and wheel upgrades cost big bucks, and for 5-liter Mustang enthusiasts on a limited budget, this isn't really a viable option.

For years, the simplest way to take advantage of slightly better brakes and a wider wheel choice was to employ Fox (1982–1987) Lincoln Continental front rotors at the front, with Aerostar van or Ranger truck axles at the back. When all was said and done, however, the advantage of doing this wasn't really that great.

Today, however, things are much improved. When Ford launched the revised SN95 Mustang for 1994, it finally gave the car an adequate four-wheel disc braking system and five-lug wheels. Mustang owners could not only stop better, they could now take full advantage of the huge selection of brake, suspension, and wheel upgrades available for five-lug applications. Today, the widespread availability of SN95 parts means that owners can perform a five-lug conversion on their 1979–1993 Mustang and gain all the advantages associated with it—including better braking and handling—for a reasonable cost.

If you're on a budget and the car on which you're performing the five-lug conversion is stock, you can reuse your existing master cylinder. However, if you upgrade to bigger aftermarket brakes, you'll need to change it. For Fox Mustangs, one of the best bets is to swap it for a 1993 Cobra master cylinder with dual ports.

Before tackling this project, you'll need a complete five-lug kit, which includes calipers, machined five-lug rotors, axles, mounting brackets, dust shields, clamps,

Because 1979–1993 5-liter Mustangs (except SVT Cobras) came with four-lug bolt pattern wheels like this, your choice of replacement wheel and brake packages is quite limited. Yet there is a way to solve this problem, and it won't cost you as much as you might think.

When doing a basic five-lug conversion with stock SN95 parts, you can retain your original Fox brake master cylinder—though if you're planning to install bigger aftermarket brakes in the future, you'll need to replace it.

The 1994–1995 Mustangs, which use five-lug wheels, have different front struts and spindles. You'll need to change these as well to get the front brakes to fit properly.

brake pads, parking brake cables, spindles, and SN95 front struts, along with all the required (and preferably new) bolts and screws.

A specialist Mustang salvage yard (such as Mustang Parts Specialties in Winder, Georgia) is an excellent place to start, especially if you're on a budget, because they can often supply everything you need, right down to replacement brake fittings. The SN95 five-lug conversion represents tremendously good value, because it uses many of your car's existing parts, though for older 1979–1986 Mustangs, you'll probably need new brake lines and fittings.

Installing the SN95 components on your Fox Mustang will change the car's tracking and steering geometry (for the better), so once the project is completed, an alignment should be on your list to make the most of the upgrade.

You'll need an extra pair of hands when doing this job, and the more experienced, the better. Jack up the car and support it on axle stands front and rear, or a lift. It's always best to tackle one wheel at a time, and the front is a logical place to start. With the wheel removed, use a 17 mm or 11/16-inch socket to remove the brake caliper, then pry off the hub dust cap with a screwdriver before removing the disc itself.

Remove the brake dust shield to access the front strut bolts and tie rod castle pins. Place a jack under the lower control arm to keep the spring compressed while you work. Use a 19 mm or 3/4-inch socket to remove the tie rod pin's castle nut. Keep the nut in place until you've removed the tie rod from the spindle, otherwise you'll

damage the tie rod shank threads. Strike the spindle on the boss using a big hammer. Several blows should be enough to free it.

If your Mustang has covered quite a few miles, now would be a good time to replace the ball joints too. (If they're stiff and difficult to move, they need replacing.) Remove the bolts that secure the spindle to the strut, and the old spindle will come right off. Remove the strut by unscrewing the three upper-mount-to-shock-tower retaining nuts, then carefully ease it out.

Install the replacement SN95 strut (making sure you use new bolts and nuts). It will secure in exactly the same location as the old strut. Once it's secured, attach your replacement SN95 spindle over the ball joint and slowly tighten the castle nut until it aligns with the hole in the tie rod shank.

Now install the new front dust shields with a rivet gun, followed by the new SN95 front hub assembly. The new hubs are permanently sealed and simply slide right over the spindles. Make sure you torque the hub's locknut to approximately 120 ft-lb and spin the hub on the spindle, to make sure it doesn't bind.

Next up is installation of the replacement SN95 front caliper. Use new pads and new or freshly machined stock

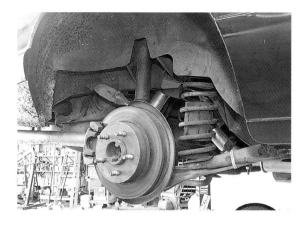

At the rear, pull out and replace the axles with those from the SN95 Mustang. Also install new brackets and fittings for your rear calipers and rear bearing/axle seals, to prevent leakage and eventual seizure. This picture shows the SN95 rear disc and caliper installed—looks factory doesn't it? *Evan Smith*

Here's our Mustang with a completed five-lug conversion. This 1987 GT has been fitted with used factory 17-inch rims from a 1999 Cobra—good for those on a budget.

SN95 rotors. The calipers should have the shims and pads already fitted before installing them. Once the caliper is fitted, drill a 3/16-inch hole on the inner frame on the driver's side to install new brake line hose brackets.

Attach the SN95 hose and bracket to the existing steel brake line. You'll probably need to cut and flare the steel tubing to do this, so use 7/16- and 11/16-inch flare fitting wrenches (in conjunction with protective gloves, to prevent spilling brake fluid on your skin). Once you've securely attached the new hose to the old brake line, reinstall the wheel bearing dust cap to complete your first of four assemblies. Tackle the other front hub assembly in the same fashion before turning to the rears.

At the back, locate the differential plug and drain the gear fluid to remove the axles. With the wheels and brake drums off, spin the differential until you find the crosspin

retaining bolt. Pull it off with a 5/16-inch socket and slide out the crosspin. Push in both axle shafts to locate and remove the C-clips. Each axle shaft will slide out.

Use a 9 /16-inch socket to undo the four bolts securing the brake drum back plate and remove it, along with the parking brake cables. Install the new SN95 caliper bracket. Bolt on the new dust shields, using a 5/16-inch socket to tighten the bolts.

Replace the outer wheel bearing seals before carefully inserting the SN95 rear axle shafts, sliding each one as far as it will go. Make sure you don't damage the seals. Put the C-clips back in place and pull the axle shafts out a little, to make sure they're secured. Put the crosspin back in and reinstall the nut. Refill the differential with oil.

Install the rear caliper bracket and check for alignment with the new caliper. Then install the new SN95 rotors. Use a lug nut or two to prevent the rotor from coming off while you're installing the calipers. Use the two bolts and corresponding 15 mm heads to secure the caliper mount and brake pads. Angle the butterfly springs up a bit to make sure the caliper will fit over the mount with no problems.

With the caliper upside down and away from the brake pads, install the top caliper bolt first, then turn the caliper over to install the bottom one. You may need to compress the caliper pistons to perform this job properly, which requires a special tool that can lock and rotate the caliper piston.

Once this is done, install the replacement parking brake cables. In most SN95 five-lug conversion kits, these will come supplied with new brackets for securing the rear axle housing that are designed to line up with the grooves in your Mustang's floorpan. The cables can then be attached to the brackets (though on some Mustangs you'll need to drill fresh holes to attach the brackets). Your new brake cables will attach to the existing balance bar of your stock Mustang's parking brake handle.

Bleed the brakes once, then after about 45 minutes, bleed it twice more, to make sure you've got all the bubbles out. Refill the master cylinder reservoir with fluid, and your five-lug conversion is done.

With the project completed, you'll notice that both front wheels are pointing inward slightly (toe in), caused by the SN95 spindles having different Ackerman angles from the old ones. To drive the car to a shop for alignment, use duct tape to mark the tie rod shafts before turning the locknuts 8–10 turns outward with a 7/8-inch wrench, to prevent uneven suspension and tire wear. Make sure you get that alignment done as soon as possible, to avoid unpredictable steering situations and excess tire wear.

SECTION 6

SUSPENSION
Projects 26-30

PROJECT 26 ★ *Installing Adjustable Camber Plates*

Time: **4 hours**

Tools: **Impact gun, wrench, adjustable torque wrench, sockets, floor jack**

Talent: ★★★

Applicable years: **All**

Tab: **$200**

Parts: **Adjustable camber plate kit**

Tip: **Make sure you carefully support the control arms, to prevent the front springs from popping out.**

Performance Improvement: **Improved handling and steering response**

Complementary Project: **Spring and shock/strut upgrade**

Like the brakes, the basic suspension on the 5-liter Fox Mustang leaves a lot to be desired. Besides the archaic rear suspension setup, a major obstacle is that these cars came from the factory with limited adjustment for camber and none for caster. The stock plates on top of the shock tower incorporate slotted holes that enable the strut to be moved to adjusting camber.

The problem is that when you lower the front end, there isn't enough camber adjustment to compensate, so the wheels adopt a pronounced negative camber (the tops of the front wheels leaning inward toward one another). On high-mileage stock 5-liters (just look at any weary mid-1980s GT or LX), the same thing tends to happen as the springs and shocks sag with age. The result is a Mustang that looks like an elephant sat on the hood and pronounced front tire wear on the inside edge, plus a car that can be all over the road at higher speeds. The problem is exaggerated by no factory provision for caster adjustment (which enables the front tires to remain fairly level when the suspension is compressed and the car is turning at speed, hence reducing wear).

To fix this irritating problem, the solution is to install adjustable camber plates. These are actually two separate plates that fit on the top of each shock tower and are linked together by clamping cap screws. Because they're separate, they allow individual adjustment of both camber and caster. Many of these plates (also known as aftermarket adjustment plates) also feature extra height for the strut mounting, which prevents the strut from bottoming out on Mustangs with lowered suspension. It keeps the strut midway through its suspension travel. These plates make a great deal of sense, especially if you plan on lowering your 5-liter in the future.

Installing adjustable camber plates is pretty straightforward. Put the Mustang on jack stands or a lift. Remove the front wheels and place another jack securely under the lower control arm. Then unbolt the brake caliper and push it aside, so you can remove the front rotor for better access to the strut.

Under the hood, use a 1/4-inch drill to remove the rivets securing the factory camber plates to the inner fender. Using a 3/4-inch socket, loosen the three remaining bolts securing the factory plates. Grab a 13/16-inch socket and loosen the top strut bolt. Also remove the strut/spindle bolts at the bottom. Carefully lowering the jack on the lower control arm (to prevent the spring from popping out), pull the strut out.

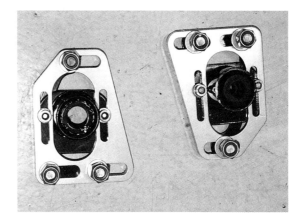

Adjustable camber plates such as these are a great solution to cure a Fox-body Mustang's front-end ailment. They enable you to adjust both caster and camber separately.

Do one side at a time and attach the bottom part of the shock tower before turning your attention to the upper part of the plate, shown here. *Evan Smith*

A major problem with Fox Mustangs from the factory is the limited camber and nonexistent caster adjustments. This leaves little remedy when handling starts to deteriorate over time and front suspension components wear out.

Install a replacement bump stop (the original will no doubt be worn and useless by this point), retaining ring, and dust boot, which you can attach to the strut using a zip tie that often comes in replacement camber-plate kits.

Install your new adjustable camber plates by placing the bottom part of the plate at the top of the shock tower, underneath the inner fender. Bolt the plate from the top side of the shock tower, using the bolts supplied. Some individuals may want to install a Heim joint or rod end bearing in place of a polyurethane bushing, but on street cars this is less than ideal. You still need some flexibility when it comes to suspension travel, otherwise your teeth will fall out every time you drive over a pothole, and the integrity of the flimsy chassis will be pushed to its limit. Polyurethane bushings are the best bet for most applications.

Before installing the strut, place at least two or three washers between the shock spacer sleeve (at the top) and the lower bushing. The reason is that the replacement plates sit taller than the stockers, as do the struts once they're mounted. Installing more washers reduces the amount of suspension travel, but it also prevents the top of the shock from hitting (and denting) the underside of the hood when the suspension is compressed.

Install the lower bushing with the flange pointing upward and the upper bushing with the flange pointing downward. Slide the strut through the camber plates and secure it. Tighten the strut/spindle nuts and secure the top strut nut. Tighten it to 30 ft-lb and the three camber plate bolts to 60 ft-lb.

You can now individually set camber and caster adjustments on your 5-liter Mustang by turning the bolts and studs—the big studs control camber; the smaller ones, caster.

PROJECT 27 ★ *Replacing the Rear Control Arms*

Time: 3 hours

Tools: Wrench, adjustable torque wrench, sockets, drill, floor jack, safety chain, grease

Talent: ★★★

Applicable years: All

Parts: Replacement control arms, bushings, bolts

Tab: $400

Tip: Install softer bushings at the upper-control-arm-to-body attachment points.

Performance Improvement: Improved traction and handling

Given that the 5-liter Mustang was derived from an economy sedan, the humble Ford Fairmont, the suspension design (both front and rear) can best be described as adequate. At the front, the car employs modified MacPherson strut geometry, while out back, a pair of short upper and longer lower control arms keep the axle in place and control front/rear and lateral movement.

The rear suspension in particular causes problems, in that the stubby upper control arms and the longer lower ones move in different arcs once the suspension is under load, especially around fairly tight corners. This produces the effect of trying to pull the axle in two directions at the same time. Not surprisingly, this puts tremendous strain on the control arms and is to a large extent responsible for the 5-liter's tricky at-the-limit handling. Because cost and compromise were of utmost importance for Ford when building these cars, the way around this problem was to use very soft bushings at the upper control arm attachment points. Over time the bushings become worn, and the control arms can distort, causing scary handling and pronounced wheel hop (even on a basically stock car with the quad shock damping).

Therefore, considering the age of most 5-liters, replacing the rear control arms is a sensible idea. Most replacement arms are thicker (and thus stronger) than the stockers and come with polyurethane bushings, which provide less flex than the stock rubber ones.

Several companies offer rear control arms tailored to your specific needs—stock, modified street, street/strip, drag or road racing. You can also buy adjustable replacement arms, such as those from Griggs Racing, that alter the length and spring height, so you can tune your suspension to suit the road and your driving conditions. The best part about these pieces is that they work with the stock rear coil springs. Although they're among the most expensive replacement control arms on the market, they're among the best, and their overall flexibility (especially when you decide to really modify your Mustang) cannot be denied.

Make sure, when installing new replacement arms (especially on a street 5-liter), that you use rubber bushings (not polyurethane) where the uppers attach to the frame. Otherwise, your Mustang's control arms will have insufficient give at the attachment points, and the back end of the car will skitter through corners and make an embarrassing creaking and groaning noise when you're turning into parking lots.

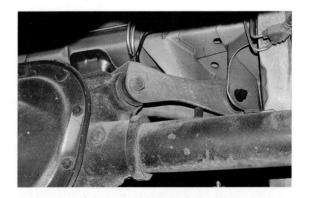

The rear suspension–specifically, the control arms on 5-liter Mustangs–isn't suitable for performance applications and is to a large extent responsible for the rear end's tendency to skitter and slide through fast corners. Shown is the factory upper arm.

SUSPENSION

The stock lowers (right side shown here) are flimsy and, under hard cornering, can eventually distort. Replacing them with stronger aftermarket units improves lateral stability and handling.

Different types of control arms are available. The red MAC lower arm shown here is great for street performance, while the black Lakewood arm is aimed more at the drag strip. Note the difference in size between the bushings.

When selecting lower control arms, consider the upgrade as part of a complete suspension package. This Lakewood arm has been supplemented with a soft-rate drag spring and shock, because this Mustang is destined to spend a considerable amount of time at the strip.

Put the car on a lift or place it on tall jack stands and block the front wheels. Place a jack under the rear axle housing, to support it. Remove the upper-arm-to-axle-pivot nut and bolt. Next, remove the corresponding frame-to-upper-arm pivot bolt. Pull off the upper arm (do one arm at a time) and test fit its replacement at the front bracket, where it attaches to the unibody. If it fits properly, secure it with a new pivot bolt and nut (but only hand tighten the bolt).

Make sure the rear of the arm properly aligns with the axle ear. If it does, install another fresh pivot bolt at the rear, where it mates with the axle, again only hand tighten. Once both arms are done, use the lift and jack to adjust the rear axle to the correct ride height. Then tighten and torque the pivot bolts to spec.

When it comes to replacing the lower control arms, things are a little more complicated. It's probably best to do the uppers first. To replace the longer arms, with the car already supported on a lift or jack stands, remove the rear wheels. Then remove the rear sway bar and put it aside, so you can remove the rear coil springs (do one side at a time). If you've never removed springs before, get some help or get a shop to do the work for you. Spring removal and installation can be quite hazardous if not performed correctly.

To remove the spring, make sure the rear axle is firmly supported, use a safety chain around the coil spring and one of the frame members. If you don't, the spring can fly out and possibly kill you. Place another jack under the lower arm pivot and remove the pivot bolt and nut. Slowly lower the jack until the spring is fully extended. Slowly pull out the spring and safety chain, followed by the rubber insulator (it will probably be worn and cracked).

Remove the pivot nut and bolt at the rear of the lower arm and then the arm itself. Align the new arm with the bracket on the frame, then install and hand tighten a new pivot bolt and nut. Install the trailing-arm pivot bolt in the same fashion (the bolts should face outward).

Do the lower arm on the other side, then carefully install new rubber isolators and your coil springs. Use the jack to move the axle up to simulate the correct ride height, so you can properly torque the pivot bolts. Then reinstall your rear sway bar and, finally, your wheels.

PROJECT 28 ★ *Lowering Your Mustang*

Time: **4 hours**

Tools: **Impact gun, adjustable torque wrench, sockets, spring compressor, safety chain, friendly assistant**

Talent: ★ ★ ★

Applicable years: **All**

Parts: **Replacement springs, shocks, front struts, stops, bushings**

Tab: **$500 (complete spring kit)**

Tip: **Install softer bushings at the upper-control-arm-to-body attachment points.**

Performance Improvement: **Improved handling, ride, looks**

Complementary Project: **Replacement shocks and a bump steer kit**

SUSPENSION

It's common practice to lower your car, for that cool, road-racer, or in-the-weeds look. However, to provide the best balance of handling and ride, this requires careful planning. Some individuals install lighter and softer-rate springs to lower their Mustangs, and although the car may look cool, it often suffers from a rock-hard ride and serious bump steer, making it a real chore to drive.

To lower one of these cars properly, certain elements must be addressed. The first one is installing adjustable camber plates (Project 26), to allow for both camber and caster adjustments. You'll also need to select the right springs and replacement bushings, followed by the right shock absorbers. Last but not least, you'll need to address the problem of bump steer, to keep the Mustang pointing in the right direction at speed and prevent it from darting all over the road.

Place the Mustang on a lift and remove the wheels. Put jacks under the front and rear lower control arms. Starting at the front, disconnect the front sway bar link to the lower control arm and install a spring compressor (available at most auto parts stores). The compressor consists of a rod, forcing nut, thrust washer, upper and lower ball nuts, a special plate, and a pin to secure it.

Install the lower plate washer, bearing, and ball nut on the rod, then slowly tighten the forcing nut just enough to feel spring pressure. Have a colleague slowly raise the car while keeping the lower arm in place. Slowly loosen the forcing nut on the compressor to relieve the spring pressure while he or she is doing this. Once the spring pressure has been relieved, remove the compressor and slowly pull the spring out.

At the back, make sure the jack is securely in place under the lower control arm. Secure a chain around the spring and disconnect the shock mounts. Slowly raise the Mustang on the lift until the control arm begins to drop. Carefully remove the spring and put it out of the way.

It's tempting to install the shortest springs you can find, but the lack of suspension travel and ultra-low ride height will contribute to a very bumpy ride and can damage the underside of your pony car. For the best overall performance gain, consider a set of variable-rate springs. These are so named because, unlike linear-rate factory springs, some of the coils are closer together than

Choosing the right spring for your Mustang hinges on a number of factors. For most street cars, a set of progressive-rate coils represent a good compromise between agile handling and compliant ride.

When pulling out your old springs, make sure the lower control arms are supported with jacks and that spring pressure is released gradually—otherwise, the spring can bounce out and cause serious damage. The sway bar link has already been disconnected.

New rubber spring bushings are a must when installing new coils, because your factory originals will often be dry-rotted and spent.

others. These closer coils soften the spring rate, while the wider-spaced coils add firmness, reduce body roll, and minimize travel when hitting large bumps and potholes. Although they don't aid handling as much as short, linear-rate springs on a pebble-smooth road surface, they provide a good compromise between cornering ability and ride. Many road-race cars fitted with short linear springs are utterly bone shaking and awful to drive at normal street speeds and conditions.

Besides a harsher ride, reduced spring height and reduced travel aren't good for drag launches—though these cars sometimes venture to the strip. To get a good hookup and good ETs, the car's rear suspension must compress on weight transfer. This is why some Fox Mustang drag cars ride on soft four-cylinder suspension.

In the 5-liter Mustang world, BBK, Steeda, and Eibach are among the most popular manufacturers of replacement springs. The Eibachs are top quality and are available in various configurations. On most street 5-liters, consider going with a 1-inch front and 3/4-inch rear

drop, which Eibach's Pro lowering springs provide. Many owners will go with a greater reduction in ride height, up to 2 inches in front, and more aggressive and stiffer springs, such as Eibach Sportlines.

You'll need new bushings. By this stage, the factory rubber spring bushings are long since worn. These bushings simply fit over the ends of each coil and are designed to prevent metal-to-metal contact between the springs, unibody, and lower control arms.

When installing new springs, reuse or install new spring dampers (the cylindrical pieces of rubber that fit inside the spring). These modulate spring compression, but if you're installing shorter (lower) springs, shorten the dampers—for 1-inch Pros, a good yardstick is cutting the factory dampers down to half size. If you don't, they'll restrict suspension travel. Also check the stops that fit between the spring, upper body, and lower control arms. Chances are they'll be worn, but luckily most spring kits come with replacements, so you can simply swap them.

PROJECT 29 ★ *Replacing the Struts and Shocks*

Time: **3 hours**

Tools: **Impact gun, wrench, adjustable torque wrench, sockets, Torx socket, floor jack**

Talent: ★ ★ ★

Applicable years: **All**

Parts: **Replacement struts, shocks, bushings**

Tab: **$400**

Tip: **Use fresh washers, bolts and bushings.**

Performance Improvement: **Improved handling and ride, decreased stopping distance**

If you're going ahead with replacement springs, consider installing new struts/shocks too. The shock absorbers control or dampen spring movement. If you install stiffer replacement springs and keep the stock struts and shocks, your Mustang will bounce up and down like a yo-yo, and the advantages offered by progressive- (variable-) rate springs won't be properly exploited. Shocks also have a great deal of influence on ride and even stopping distance when you hit the brakes.

Combining good-quality up-rated shocks with replacement springs will result in a 5-liter that is both a capable handler in most situations yet compliant and safe to drive on a daily basis. The factory gas-charged shocks installed from 1985 and up aren't bad, but they do wear out and sag over the years, causing the car to develop a "natural" lowered stance.

Replacement shocks are widely available through the aftermarket. Bilstein, Koni, and Tokico are among the best-quality replacements out there. Many owners on a budget go with adjustable KYBs, which are cheaper and aren't bad. Most shocks designed for street 5-liters are nonadjustable, though a number of adjustable shocks (up to 7-way) are available. Those with the greater number of adjustments are aimed more at road racers who wish to tweak every last inch of their suspension settings.

To remove and install new front struts, follow a path similar to installing new camber plates. Begin by removing the front rotor and caliper; push the latter aside. Secure the lower control arm with a jack. Unscrew the three retaining bolts on the camber plate that hold the strut in place at the top (see Project 26) and the bolts that secure it to the spindle. You can now pull it out. If you're installing new front struts, remove and swap over or install a new upper mount. Do this by unfastening the bolt on the top of the strut. The upper mount then slides off.

Strut and spring replacement go hand in hand. As when selecting replacement coils, selecting the proper struts and shocks hinges on your requirements. Although the factory shocks aren't bad, aftermarket replacements, such as these Tokicos, can take handling to an entirely different level.

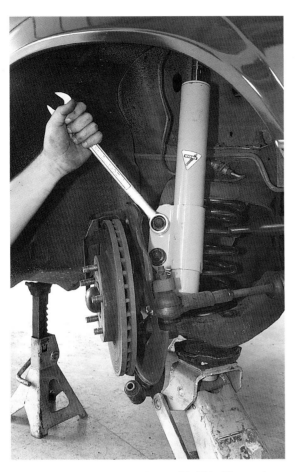

For the rear shocks (we're talking the vertical, not the horizontal ones found on 1984–1995 cars—the latter are cheap and easy to replace, costing $30 or less) as with the fronts, support the lower control arms with a jack once the car is up on the lift. Pop open the trunk and access the shock upper mounting nuts beneath the carpet (on two-door models) or under those plastic fender inspection covers aft of the quarter windows on hatchback Mustangs. Carefully loosen and remove the upper mounting nut with a wrench. For the bottom, you'll need a special Torx socket to remove the mounting bolts—if you don't, you'll strip the bolt heads. Ease the shock out from under the car.

When upgrading struts and shocks, use harder, polyurethane bushings, especially at the front—they reduce unwanted suspension travel and tighten up the front end, for improved handling. Also install fresh washers and bolts along with the insulator bushings.

Once the new struts and shocks have been installed, put your new springs in place. The pigtails at the bottom of the front springs should cover only one of the two drain holes where they attach to the control arm. The pigtails on the rear springs, where they meet the lower control arms, should point toward the left side of the car.

Have somebody with considerable experience working on and tuning Mustangs check over the installation, because any problems can become a major safety hazard. If everything is okay, it's time to turn your attention to bump steer.

Because 5-liter Mustangs employ modified MacPherson front suspension, removing and installing your new front struts is fairly simple. Support the lower control arm with a jack, to keep the spring in place.

From mid-1984, 5-liter Mustangs employed a secondary pair of horizontal shocks to control wheel hop, as opposed to traction bars found on 1979 to early 1984 models. When upgrading your vertical rear shocks, consider replacing these too, because they're fairly cheap insurance. *Evan Smith*

PROJECT 30 ★ *Addressing Bump Steer*

Time: **2 hours**

Tools: **Wrench, adjustable torque wrench, sockets, soft hammer**

Talent: ★★

Applicable years: **All**

Parts: **Offset rack bushings, replacement tie rod ends and spacers**

Tab: **$400**

Tip: **Get to the alignment shop as soon as you're done.**

Performance Improvement: **Improved steering response, feel, safety, better handling**

Complementary Project: **Adjustable camber plates**

You'll hear the term "bump steer" a lot when discussing suspension upgrades, and it's something that must be addressed. When you lower your Mustang—even by an inch in ride height—you automatically change the suspension geometry. As mentioned previously, adjustable camber plates will help correct the angle of the front wheels, but lowering still upsets your 5-liter's steering geometry.

Once the vehicle is dropped from its stock ride height, the tie rod ends now point upward to mate with the steering rack, instead of being even with it. When the suspension extends and compresses, the tie rods move in different arcs, causing the front wheels to freely move without your steering input every time you hit an imperfection in the road—hence "bump steer." This causes darting and unpredictable street manners and can be downright scary through a high-speed corner.

Curing this potentially hazardous problem can be done in a couple of ways.

Arguably the cheapest and most popular method is to swap the stock steering-rack bushings with offset replacements. These bushings are found at the bottom of the steering rack, where it bolts to the front of the K-member. To get to the bushings, remove the rack from the car. Remove the front wheels, rotors and calipers, and pull off the tie rod ends from the spindles. To do this, loosen the nuts on top of each tie rod (one at a time), then use a hammer to hit the side of the spindle. The pin should come out after a few light blows.

Support the steering gear, so you don't damage the linkage. Once it's secure, remove the bolts that hold the rack to the K-member. Pull the bushings out from the rear of the rack, along with the washers that attach at the front. Install the offset replacement bushings in the same location, along with the washers and bolts. Offset bushings are so named because they have off-center holes,

Installing lowering springs changes the front end of your suspension geometry , so you'll need to prevent bump steer. You can do this a couple of ways, though offset bushings such as these are a good place to start.

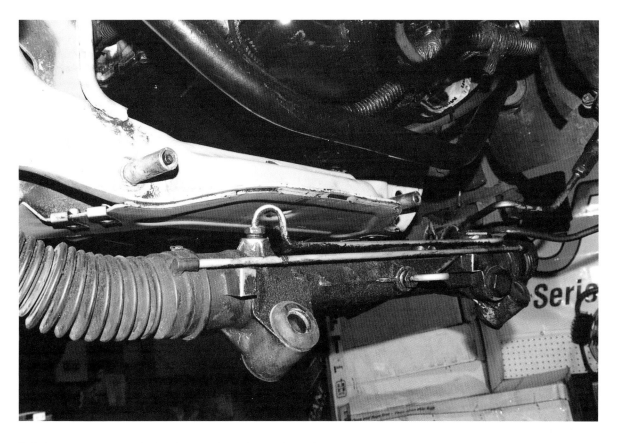

With the steering rack unbolted and dropped from the front K-member, you can see the bushings and the mounts onto which they secure. There are four bushings, two on each side of the rack. Pull them out and install your replacements.

which enable you to raise and lower the steering rack to compensate for changes in ride height.

The other—and, some may say, more effective—solution (particularly on significantly lowered Mustangs) is to install a bump steer correction kit, though if you're fitting tires much bigger than stock, it would be wise to perform both the rack bushing replacement and bump steer kit install.

The latter consists of adjustable replacement tie rod ends and a pair of spacers that attach between the spindles and tie rod ends. To install them, loosen the inner jam nut so you can remove your stock outer tie rods, using another wrench to grip the rod while you loosen the nut. Carefully unthread the rod and pull it off.

Install the tapered shanks and spacers that come supplied with the kit into the spindle end. The medium-sized spacers should be located at the top of the shank, with the others at the bottom. Torque the top and bottom nuts to specs: 40 ft-lb up top and 50 ft-lb at the bottom.

Once you've completed this project, get your Mustang to the alignment shop pronto, so they can check the installation and make any adjustments required.

93

PROJECT 31 ★   *Installing a New Convertible Top*

Time: 5 hours

Tools: **Flat-blade and Phillips-head screwdrivers, heavy-duty cloth, wrench, torque wrench, 13 mm deep socket, industrial tape, staple gun, trim adhesive glue**

Talent: ★★★

Applicable years: 1983–1995 Mustang convertibles

Tab: $300

Parts: New sail cloth top, bolts and screws

Tip: Keep the ends of the tension cables outside the body at all times.

Performance Improvement: A top that looks good and doesn't leak

Complementary Project: Replace the glass rear window and latch mechanism

In 1983, after an absence of 10 years, Ford reintroduced the soft-top body style to the Mustang lineup. Initially only available in glitzy GLX trim, complete with wood veneer interior paneling, it soon became available in both regular and high-performance GT trim and continues to this day. Many of these once pristine tops are ripped, have broken fittings and perished seals, or are just plain ratty. Admit it—nobody wants to drive a convertible with a top that leaks, doesn't work properly, or looks like it sat under a tree for five years.

The solution is to install a replacement, and thanks to burgeoning aftermarket support, new tops are readily available. The original Ford tops were made from "sail cloth" single-texture vinyl. For best results and that clean OEM look, stick to this material, which is surprisingly hard wearing. Among the vendors offering replacement tops, Texas-based Latemodel Restoration Supply has carved itself a special niche with quality replacement 5-liter tops. The company also sells otherwise hard-to-find pieces, including the zip-out glass rear window, latches, and top motor and cylinder, along with replacement top boots and even the quarter-window motor.

It's best to do this job inside, because installing a top is quite fiddly, and you'll want as few distractions and as little interference from the elements as possible. Take a good look at the overall condition of the top by walking around the car. All factory 5-liter Mustang ragtops were of the power hydraulic variety, activated by a button on the dash (early cars) or on the center console (latter examples). Examine the top itself, the frame, and the mechani-

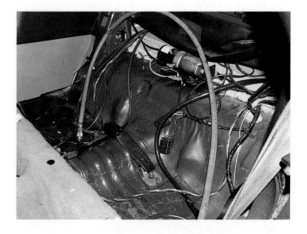

Not as difficult a project as you might think, installing a convertible top is quite straightforward, provided you take your time. One of the first things is to remove the rear seat.

cals, in both the up and down positions, to be sure you get everything that needs fixing done at once. Before starting, make sure the bodywork of the car is thoroughly protected by covering it in thick cloth and taping it securely to the coachwork, to prevent damaging or scratching it. Another good idea is to remove the rear seat.

Undo the retainers that secure the top to the windshield header in the up position, then press the button to lower the top just a touch. Remove the header plate (it's secured by screws) and put it in a safe place. Slowly separate the top from the headlining underneath and disconnect the metal tubes and tabs that secure it to the top frame. (The top is prepunched and has plastic tabs that snap it into place over the frame.)

Disconnect the tension cables, which run on each side between the windows and top seals, by unfastening the tabs that secure them near the quarter windows at the back. Be careful when doing this. If the cables fall down between the quarter windows and interior panels, you'll need to remove the rear seat (if you haven't already) and the panels to get at them (a lengthy, irritating task). Carefully rest the cable ends on the edge of the bodywork, by the windows. When replacing a convertible top that has been subject only to regular wear and tear, the headlining is usually in pretty good shape and can be reused.

Pull out the metal reinforcements for the convertible frame and check for alignment and condition. In most instances they should be okay. Disconnect the top from around the rear window and boot area by pulling out the staples that secure it. Use a 12 or 13 mm deep socket to take off the tabs for the liner inside the boot well. Then you can pull off the old, battered top and throw it away.

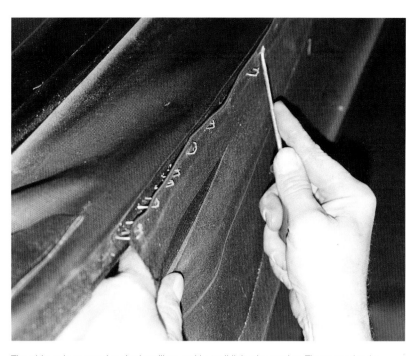

The old top is secured to the headliner and its well lining by staples. These need to be removed so you can pull the old top off and away from the well lining and tip frame.

Replacement tops are becoming increasingly available through the aftermarket. For best results, use a quality top manufactured from single texture sail cloth like the OEM original.

The older Fox Mustangs are trickier to work on than the 1994-95 cars, because the weaker chassis has a tendency to bend and twist. This puts greater stress on the

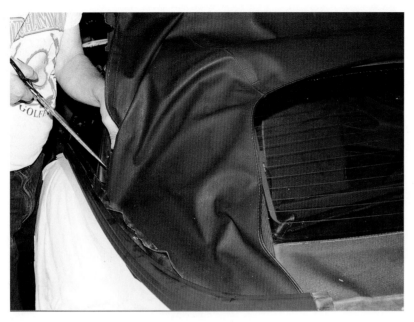

Once the new top is attached to the frame mechanism, trim off excess material, particularly around the boot well lining and rear window, to provide a neat, exact fit.

convertible frame, making it harder to get the replacement top to fit properly, especially at the windshield header. From 1990, Ford also revised the top stowing mechanism, reducing the height of the top—something worth bearing in mind when selecting a replacement roof. However, according to Toronto-based New Image interiors, a company that has replaced many tops, when all is said and done, the installation procedure for both the Fox and SN95 Mustangs is pretty much the same.

To install the new top, drape it over the frame, then attach the snap tabs to the rear frame crossmember. Install the headliner tabs over it and secure the headliner firmly with screws. Get out your measuring tape and make sure the bridge mount on the top corresponds to the rear crossmember and the bottom of the frame by the rear window. If it doesn't, your new top won't fit properly.

If everything checks out, use an air staple gun to secure the top to the frame (except at the front by the headliner). Then mark the front staple tab and measure the distance to the windshield header before using an air staple gun to secure the front portion of the top underside to the frame. Slide the metal stiffener into the convertible top mounting sleeve before stapling the top to the frame.

Next up are the tension cables on each side. Place the tension wires on the frame by the rear quarter windows.

Staple the top fabric around the edge of the rear window and boot. Make sure the tension of the fabric is correct around the rear window (no wrinkles, etc.) and trim off the excess material around the edge. Pull the bottom end of the top into the boot well—it should line up with the plastic tabs and slot in place at the edge, where the top meets the boot well.

Turn on the ignition and press the button to move the top mechanism forward, until it's about an inch from the windshield header. Reinstall the cable tension wires on each side. Carefully work on one at a time and slide them through the sleeves in the top on each side, on the side of the frame just above the windows. Pull each tensioner up and through the points at the quarter windows and secure them at the front—this will help keep the top tight when it's raised or lowered.

Slide the rearmost portion of the top into place under the boot sills—it simply bolts in. Reinstall the plastic boot trim over the top of the fabric, and snap on the boot well liner. Then screw in the retainers around the quarter windows and snap in the rubber headliner seals over them (there should be three bolts and four retainers).

The next step is to glue and secure the top around the front at the header panel. Before doing this, however, checking the tension of the top is a must (staple it to the header panel first, to make sure it's tight before beginning the gluing). If the tension is good, mark with a piece of chalk 1/2 inch behind the header panel. This should make the top fit exactly right—any less than 1/2 inch and the top will be too loose; any more and it will put excess pressure on the rear window area when the top is raised. Remove the staples and glue the header panel with trim adhesive.

Once you're done, reinstall the header panel screws and inspect the top and trim for fit. Carefully trim off any excess material. Raise and lower the top a few times, to make sure the mechanism works properly, the tension is good, and that the top fabric doesn't get caught on anything. If all is well, your new convertible top will make your decade-old Mustang look years younger.

PROJECT 32 ★ *Repairing the Front Fascia and Rear Bumper*

Time: 15 hours (prep work)

Tools: Adjustable torque wrench, sockets, jig, TPO plastic repair kit, instant glue, adhesion activator, sander, sandpaper (different grits), flashlight, reputable paint shop

Talent: ★ ★ ★ ★

Applicable years: 1979–1993 (1994–1995 similar)

Tab: $1,200

Parts: N/A

Tip: Take your time doing the prep work, and make sure you get a good body shop to paint the parts.

Performance Improvement: Showroom-quality bumpers without fit problems

Complementary Project: Repainting the rest of the Mustang

Parking lot scrapes, road debris, and the weather all conspire to turn the exterior of your once pristine Mustang into something fit for the local speedway. One of the most common areas of bodywork to suffer from these blues is the front and rear fascias, or bumper covers.

Like most Detroit vehicles with their origins in the late 1970s, the 5-liter Mustang has big 5-mph steel bumpers mounted on massive rams, to withstand low-speed shunts. Over the bumpers were mounted a urethane front and rear cap that blended with the body contours. If the Mustang was hit at speeds below 5 mph, not only would the steel bumpers return to their original position, but the flexible urethane plastic would also return to its original shape. However, Fox Mustangs in particular are not getting any younger, and over time the urethane loses it flexibility and becomes brittle and prone to cracking.

Another problem is that the factory-applied paint—especially pre-1990 models, which didn't use clear coat—starts to fade, and with the plastic beneath it changing structure, tends to flake and peel off. The front and rear fascias bear the brunt of kicked-up road debris and the actions of careless motorists—scrapes, scuffs, gouges, and even cracks are common, especially on regularly driven 5-liters. So if your car is starting to look a little unsightly at the front and back or at the rocker panels (on 1987–1993 GTs), here's what you can do to remedy the situation.

On 1987 and newer cars, depending on the level of damage, you can strip the bumper cover down to its bare urethane surface and repaint it, or you can install brand-new covers and prep and paint them. On 1987–1993 GTs, the rocker panel extensions are secured by small pieces of steel that you need to carefully remove to pull off the extensions. If you're doing the rocker panels, check the condition of the steel retainers—some of them will probably be bent or rusted and should be replaced.

If you own a 1979–1986 Mustang, things are a little more difficult. Aftermarket replacement bumper covers

Plastic flexible bumpers often bear the brunt of road debris. Scrapes, scratches, and even cracks are all too common on 5-liter Mustangs. If the plastic bumper covers have been repainted without using specially formulated paint, the finish will peel and crack too. This one is suffering a combination of all four of the problems mentioned.

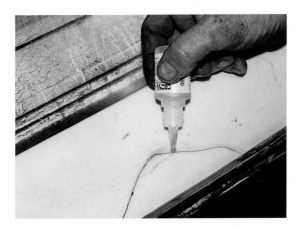

With the bumper cover removed, the repair process can begin. One of the first jobs is using a strong adhesive to fix any cracks.

For fixing cracks or blemishes in flexible plastic bumpers, use a special repair kit, such as 3M Automix, shown here.

for 1979–1982 models are nonexistent. You'll need to source a NOS (new old stock) piece or a quality used one. Usually the only way to find one is via a swap meet or a Mustang salvage yard. If you have a 1983–1984 GT or 1983–1986 LX, you can obtain a new front cover but not a rear one. If you have a 1985–1986 GT, much as with 1979–1982, you'll have to go the swap-meet and salvage-yard route.

If the surface of your cover contains minor cracks, crazing, flaking paint, and scrapes, it's probably cheaper to strip it down and repaint it than fork out for a new one. You'll be surprised at the results you can get from what appears to be a cover fit for the trash. Repairing and bringing your bumper covers back to showroom condition takes time and a lot of preparation. Although the paint application is best left to a professional, there's no reason you can't do the preparation work on the bumper cover yourself.

The first thing to do is find a place to work—a garage, or better still, a friend's body shop. Don't try this outside, even if you live in southern California or someplace else where it's sunny and 75 degrees every day of the year. Also find someone experienced in plastic body repairs for questions or supervision, especially if you have limited bodywork experience.

If you're doing the rear bumper, bring the car in and support the rear on axle stands. If you're doing the front one, jack up the front of the car. Use a torque wrench and deep socket to remove the bolts that secure the bumper cover. The rear has three on each side: two at the bottom near the tailpipes and the third in the trunk floor by the taillights (you'll probably need a flashlight to locate this one). On 1987–1993 GTs, 11 stud fasteners and four clips fasten the lower part of the rear bumper

valance to the support brackets and need to be removed before the cover can be pulled off.

For the front cover, unfasten the nuts at the back on each side that secure the cover to the fenders. Undo the rivets that hold it to the front bulkhead at the top and the bolts that fasten it to the bottom. On 1979–1986 cars, you'll find four rivets at the top and four bolts at the bottom. On 1987–1993 models, 17 small rivets attach the cover to the radiator support at the top and bottom of the headlight pockets, along with a couple of push nuts on each side that fasten the cover to the lower fender. Once you've done this, you can pull the cover off.

Now the real work begins. If you're using your existing bumper cover and it has any cracks, put it in a jig and line them up properly, so you can repair and fill them. Use a strong adhesive, like Instabond, to weld the cracks and restore the cover's integrity. Let the cover set for at least an hour.

Once the glue is set, you can start sanding. Use 80 grit to remove the weld imperfections, until the surface is smooth. Turn the cover over and do the inside as well.

Spray on an adhesive activator once you're done, to strengthen the welds. Let this set for a good 15–20 minutes before adding the epoxy adhesive. This is necessary to cover cracks and prevent them from reappearing. A good adhesive is DuPont's Flexible Parts Repair Squeeze kit. It comes in two tubes, one black, and one white. You mix both substances together until you get a consistent medium-gray color. When you do, paste the adhesive onto both sides of the damaged area of your cover, using a spatula. Once the affected area has been covered, let the paste set for at least an hour.

When the repair area is dry, reinstall the bumper cover on the car, so it doesn't flex and damage the repair. If you're doing the front fascia on a 1984–1993 GT Mustang, remove the foglights and mask around the housing. Using 80 grit, begin dry sanding the repair area, then do the rest of the cover to remove any paint and major blemishes. Follow it with another round of 80 grit, then 120, then 180, to get rid of the stress cracks, and finally 320, to get in really tight areas (including the trim indentations) and remove the smallest blemishes. You'll be glad you did this once the bumper enters the painting stage.

Your fixed bumper is now ready for paint application. When getting bumper covers done (and the rest of the car, for that matter) use a reputable body repair shop—don't go with the cheapest. A number of special substances are required to paint plastic body parts properly and prevent the paint from peeling and crazing. Although you won't often be doing this part of the project yourself, it's worth noting what's required to produce a quality, long-lasting result.

Before anything, the shop should carefully mask off the area around the bumper (you don't want primer or paint getting anywhere it shouldn't). They should also use an adhesion promoter, which is sprayed on the bumper cover to help the primer and paint stick to the plastic surface and prevent it from peeling off. One of the best is Dupont's 2330S Plas-Stick. It should be sprayed over the entire cover and allowed to set for at least 40 minutes.

Once the adhesion promoter has set, the primer can be applied. A good-quality primer should be mixed with an activator, primer converter, and drying accelerator. For best results, apply at least three or four coats of this mix to the cover. Dry sand the cover between each coat with 600 grain. Before sanding the last couple of coats, get a trained body person to look for any small indentations and fill them. A painted bumper with lots of little dimples is unsightly and frustrating.

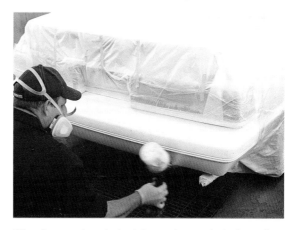

When it comes to actual painting, unless you're in the trade yourself, it's best to farm out the work to a good, reputable paint shop for quality, long-lasting results.

You'll be amazed at what's possible. The once tatty, cracked front fascia on your 1987 GT can emerge as good as new.

Now it's time for painting. Paint has come a long way since the old days of lacquer finishes. For plastic parts, especially if the Mustang is going to be driven, consider an acrylic urethane or similar paint that's hard, durable stuff and flexible enough to withstand stone chips and other maladies. The brand of paint is largely a personal preference, though DuPont is a popular and good choice among those in the trade. Once the paint shop has finished your bumper—for good results, at least a day in the paint shop is required—you'll be really glad you did all that prep work, and nobody at the cruise night or show field will ever know there's a 15-to-20-year-old bumper cover beneath that glossy paint.

PROJECT 33 ★ Installing New Headlights and Foglights

Time: 3 hours

Tools: Flat-blade and Phillips-head screwdrivers, wrench, torque wrench, sockets

Talent: ★★

Applicable years: 1987–1995

Tab: $350

Parts: New headlight and front foglight assembly

Tip: Install the corner and running lights before doing the headlamp assemblies.

Performance Improvement: Improved looks and night visibility

A common problem on 1987–1993 Mustangs—and the 1994–1995 versions, for that matter—is the so-called "yellowing" of the headlight lenses. When Ford updated the front end of the 5-liter Mustang for 1987, all models went to flush "aero" headlights, flanked by triangular turn signal/running lights and, on the outside, parking/side marker units that wrapped around the corners of the front fenders. Yellowing, old headlights not only make your Mustang look unkempt, they also reduce visibility at night. The 1994–1995 Mustangs are also starting to suffer from the same problem as they get older.

Some people try to buff the surface of the lens to bring back the original shine, but this produces questionable results. The best bet is to install a full set of replacement units, which isn't as difficult or as expensive as you might think. Since the late 1990s, the aftermarket has started to embrace restoration as well as go-faster parts for 5-liter Mustangs. Latemodel Restoration Supply is among the leading sources for replacement lenses, and with custom lighting all the rage, you can get not only OEM-style lenses with factory-style amber side markers but also clear corners, projector-style headlight units, and even diamond-cut-style or tinted-smoke units.

On 1987–1993 Mustangs, the full headlight assembly consists of six separate pieces (a corner lens, headlight lens, and turn signal/running light unit on each side), which can be purchased separately or all together. The 1994–1995 cars have two separate pieces, one for the headlight and turn signal/running light.

Unlike the 1979–1986 Mustangs, where you just pull out the entire headlight unit, secured in the bezel by four screws, you can remove the bulbs separately on the newer

cars. To do this, disconnect the negative battery cable, then access the electrical connector at the back of the bulb of the unit you wish to remove. Unplug the connector and turn the retainer that secures the bulb in the socket counterclockwise, until you can pull the bulb out. Protect the paintwork around the lens housing with cloth and tape. Locate the screws that secure the light housing and lens to the grille reinforcement panel and unfasten them, so you can pull the housing forward and out of the fascia.

Your replacement housing, whether OEM or aftermarket, will install in exactly the reverse fashion of removing your old one. It's much easier to install the side marker and turn signal lenses first. Also, try to preset the headlamp aim before installing the headlight units, because it will save you time when you adjust the beam. To do it properly, test fit the headlights. (Park the Mustang

"Yellowing" of the headlight lenses is a common problem on 1987–1993 Mustangs and also on 1994–1995 models. It's easy to change your old lenses for new ones such as this.

Replacing the headlight lenses on 1987–1993 Mustangs is slightly different from the process on earlier cars but still straightforward. First, pull the bulbs out of the socket, so you can unscrew and remove the housing.

Broken foglights are all too common on Fox Mustang GTs. The rectangular Marchal lamps on 1984–1986 models are scarce and can be costly (up to $200 apiece).

facing a wall, so you can aim the beam properly.) The adjusters are on the back of each headlight bucket.

Front Foglights

Take a good look at the front of a 1984–1993 Mustang GT the next time you come across one. If the car has been driven regularly, chances are the front foglights will be damaged or missing. These bulbs aren't an essential part of your Mustang, so it's not surprising they get neglected. But why are they such a problem?

The location of the foglamps means they bear the brunt of road debris, which defaces, cracks, and even breaks the lenses, allowing moisture to seep in and ruin the housing and bulbs. If you race your Mustang at the track and are looking to run quicker ETs, removing the foglights will save a bit of weight—and who needs to put them back in afterward, because it'll only make your car slower, right?

Clear corner lenses are all the rage for a custom look. This corner, from American Products Company (APC), is among the most stylized out there and is a direct replacement for the factory amber lens.

If you drive your 1984–1993 GT on the street, however, or are looking at entering the car in shows, a pristine set of foglamps will enhance nighttime driving and the appearance of your car's front-end. If you own a 1979–1986 Mustang, which originally came with the French Marchal driving lamps, this can be a bit of a problem. It's been almost a decade since Ford stopped carrying them in its parts inventory, and the aftermarket has yet to supply replacements in decent numbers. Many owners of these cars stick in aftermarket units that are either too big or too small for the openings and somehow just don't look right. Luckily, Latemodel Restoration Supply has begun to address the problem by introducing replacement lenses for these foglights, which makes our job of replacing the worn-out originals a little easier.

Each foglight is held in place by two screws, one on each side. Undo the screws and pull the foglight off the lower front fascia frame to which it's secured. At the back of the housing, you will find another pair of screws that secure the lens to the bucket—unfasten them and the lens comes right off. To replace the bulb, unfasten the clip on the back of the housing bucket, rotate the bulb, and pull it out of its housing.

If you own a 1987–1993 GT, you're in a much better position. Replacement circular lenses and bulbs are widely available through aftermarket vendors, and you can still buy them in limited quantities through your Ford dealership. Much like the headlights on these cars, the bulbs slot in through the back of the housing. Pull off the electrical connector and rotate the locking retainer, so you can pull the bulb out. The housing is held in place by screws. The lens assembly is retained by clips, which must be unfastened so you can pull the assembly out of the lower fascia.

SECTION 8

INTERIOR

Projects 34-35

PROJECT 34 ★ *Replacing the Seats*

Time: 3 hours

Tools: Screwdriver, wrench, adjustable torque wrench, sockets

Talent: ★★

Applicable years: All

Parts: New seats, mounting hardware, bolts, screws, pins

Tab: $0–$1,000

Tip: Test fit the seats before installing them.

Performance Improvement: Improved comfort, safety, aesthetics

Complementary Project: New interior carpet

When you're looking to buy a 5-liter Mustang, it's worth examining the condition of the interior, and especially the front seats.

You may also come across a driver's seat that's bent (particularly on LX and 1987–1993 GT 'Stangs). The reason for this is that the seat rails, frames, and attachment points are flimsy. Hard driving, combined with a pilot of considerable mass, will cause the seat to twist and bend.

Even if the rest of the car is in good shape, a ratty interior and worn seating will detract from it and should be one of the first things on your to-do list. As with most things in life, a huge variety of choice and budget is available when it comes to replacing seats. If funds are tight, consider going with a pair of low-mileage stockers, either from the same year and model or from a different one.

During the 5-liter Mustang's production run, various seats were available. Most of the Fox Mustangs built through 1988 came with low-rent and low-back adjustable semi-bucket seats with small headrests. They offer little in the way of support, though genuine Recaro adjustable sports seats were available from 1979–1982 (and are exceedingly hard to find these days).

When the GT model was mildly face-lifted for 1983, the Recaros were replaced by Ford's own sport seats of a similar design, which continued through the end of Fox

production, also becoming standard in LX 5.0s from 1989 and adopting power controls. When the SN95 Mustang was launched for 1994, it too received bucket seats, which were much stronger and more supportive than those found in its predecessor.

One of the most popular seats in street 5-liter Mustangs is the multi-adjustable sport bucket originally installed in 1985–1986 GT models. This is among the most comfy factory buckets ever installed in these cars, though good ones can be hard to find.

102

Today, decent stock Mustang seats are readily available through specialist suppliers, Mustang shops, swap meets, or even junkyards. If you're looking for everyday comfort and support, most enthusiasts recommend either a set of SN95 front buckets (widely available) or the articulated sports seats with the red piping found in 1985–1986 GTs. The latter are still popular, but due to demand (especially those headrests), price is rising, and good-quality examples are becoming scarce. (These seats also came in mid-1980s Escort GTs and EXPs.)

To remove the seats, remove the seat-track retaining bolts and nuts. If your Mustang has power seat controls, disconnect the electrical leads. Then lift the seat and track assembly out.

Unless the new seats are identical to the old ones, use the seat brackets that come with them, to make installation as painless as possible. Some aftermarket chairs feature custom brackets and Allen bolts that enable you to use the stock mounting hardware from the originals with your snazzy new seats—something worth considering, especially if you're forking out a sizable amount of cash.

A set of Ford or aftermarket seats will usually come with all the necessary brackets and fittings. Test fit the replacement seats, because some may not provide the right amount of clearance between the center console and door panel, causing rubbing and making adjustment fore and aft on the rails a pain. When you begin installation, be careful, especially with the seat-back locking mechanisms, which can easily bend and snap.

Once you've installed the seats, carefully tighten all the bolts and fittings to prevent them coming loose, and make sure the electrical connectors for the power controls are properly hooked up (if the car has them). Your new seats should make your Mustang's office a much nicer place to inhabit.

Sometimes you may want to replace the rear seat too, especially if it's a little ratty and worn, ripped, or stained. On 1979–1986 coupes and 1983–1986 convertibles, remove the screws that secure the seat cushion to the floor and then lift out the seat, followed by the seat back. On 1987–1993 coupes and convertibles, things are a little more complicated. Press downward on the seat cushion and push it backward—it slots out from supports on either side. You can then pull the cushion out. If the Mustang has those little quarter armrests, take one out to remove the seat back. Then remove the screws that secure the seat back in place, lift it up, and pull it out of the car.

On hatchback Mustangs, the seats must be in their folded position so you can pull out the five pins that attach the rear trunk carpet area to the rear seat back. Next, locate and remove the three screws that attach the folding arm to the seat backs. Then slide the rear seat off

Shown here is a typical early-1990s Mustang interior with the factory-adjustable buckets. These are prone to fabric wear (note the driver's cushion) and bending, because of the flimsy rail supports. If you're building a street machine on a budget, consider replacing them with a set of SN95 front chairs.

Removing the seats on Fox Mustangs is easy—they're secured to the floor by four bolts.

its pivot and remove it from the car. Some hatchback owners may want to leave the back seat out and cover the space with some interior automotive carpet, cut to fit. This may be especially useful if you're planning to build a killer show car with a monster sound system or eventually want to do a spot of serious road or drag racing, where a roll cage is required and a back seat just gets in the way.

PROJECT 35 ★ *Replacing the Heater Core*

Time: 2 hours (7 with air conditioning)

Tools: Flat-blade and Phillips-head screwdrivers, torque wrench, sockets

Talent: ★ ★ ★

Applicable years: All

Parts: Heater core, piping, screws

Tab: $150–$450

Tip: If you have an air-conditioned car, get this done professionally.

Performance Improvement: Warm cabin and windows that don't mist up

If you own a Fox Mustang, one thing that will probably need attention sooner or later is the heater core. The heating system in these cars operates by a heater core through which heated engine coolant passes. A blower fan activated by levers (on 1979–1986 cars) or rotating knobs (on 1987–1993) control temperature and ventilation inside the cabin.

If your Mustang has air conditioning, it also has a condenser fitted in front of the stock radiator and an evaporator mounted close to the heater core. An engine-mounted compressor, driven by a serpentine belt and located above the power steering pump, distributes the charge through a massive pipe assembly. An accumulator contains a pressure relief valve and is plumbed into the system. Unlike non-air cars, the blower fan in air-conditioned Mustangs pushes the hot cabin air through the evaporator, which transfers the heat from the air to the refrigerant (all Fox Mustangs originally used R12, which today is hard to come by). The heat causes the refrigerant to turn into low-pressure vapor, which dissipates the heat.

Over time, the heater core corrodes and breaks down internally, causing your windows to fog up on damp or cold days and coolant to seep out and ruin your carpet, giving your interior the wonderful scent of antifreeze. In northern climes, many who drive their Mustangs only during the warmer months bypass the heater core by pulling out the firewall hoses from the heater tubes and installing a U-shaped hose on the end of the intake heater tube, to reroute the flow of coolant. However, on some days, having only cold air is a bit of pain, and to be honest, you should replace your heater core, because it will affect your Mustang's resale value.

Replacing the heater core on air-conditioned cars requires taking the entire dashboard apart, but if you have a 1979–1986 Mustang that didn't come with air conditioning, you're in luck. On these cars, you can replace the heater core pretty easily yourself.

Place a protective mat on the interior carpet, then drain the cooling system, to prevent even more coolant seeping out. Loosen the two clips that secure the twin hoses to the heater core tubes at the center right side of the firewall and plug the hoses, to prevent leakage.

Inside the cabin, move the temperature lever to the hot setting at the top. Remove the glove box door by

A faulty or leaking heater core is almost guaranteed on any Fox Mustang these days, even if the car has been looked after. This one, from a 1986 GT, has corroded internally, causing coolant to seep out. New cores themselves are inexpensive, but on air-conditioned and 1987–1993 Mustangs, installation is labor-intensive.

INTERIOR

On 1979–1986 Mustangs without air, you can unscrew your glove box door and pull it off so you can access the heater core case behind it.

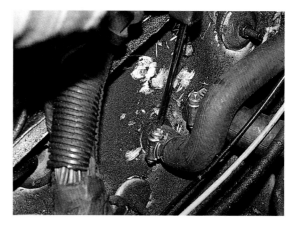

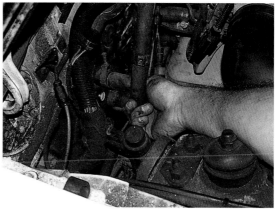

Reconnect the inlet and return tubes to the core from the coolant tubes on the intake manifold once you've installed your new heater core. Check that the tubes are secure, to prevent leakage.

unfastening the screws, then remove the vertically mounted cowl-to-instrument brace. Unfasten the four bolts that secure the heater core and pull the core cover out through the open glove box door.

Under the hood, access the three studs on the firewall that secure the heater core case. Push on the tubes to loosen the heater core, then go back inside and pull it through the glove box opening.

Installing a new heater core is the reverse of removing the old one. Once you've completed the project, refill the engine with coolant and check for any leaks.

If you own a 1979–1986 air-conditioned Mustang or a 1987–1993 car, you're in an entirely different ballgame. It's probably best to have a professional shop perform a heater core replacement. Aside from having to take the entire dash apart, you'll need to have the air conditioning system fully discharged before you can begin.

Even if you own a 1987–1993 Mustang without air, don't think you're in luck. Because many of these cars were fitted with air conditioning, Ford standardized the layout of the heater components to expedite assembly. Therefore, you'll still have to take the dash apart to replace your core. From this you can see that replacing something as simple as a lousy heater core isn't easy. To quote legendary Mustang shop owner and racer Joe Da Silva, "I love working on 5-liter Mustangs, with the exception of two things. One is changing pedals; the other, a heater core."

Although it may cost you $300–$400 to have your heater core replaced on air-equipped and 1987–1993 Mustangs, in the long run it's probably the best way to go, since the hassle and aggravation of trying to do this yourself isn't worth it for most people.

To give you an idea of what's involved, once the air conditioning system has been depressurized, the coolant drained, and the high/low pressure hoses plugged, you'll need to unfasten and remove the entire dashboard and center console to access the blower motor, evaporator case (if equipped with air), and heater core. The electrical connectors for the blower and resistor must then be removed, along with the evaporator case, heater core case, and, of course, the core from within the case.

PROJECT 36 ★ Selecting the Right Wheels and Tires

Time: As long as it takes

Tools: N/A

Talent: N/A

Applicable years: All

Tab: $100–$6,000

Parts: New wheels and tires

Tip: Speak with a tire and wheel specialist for best results and get him or her to test fit some wheel and tire combinations.

Performance Improvement: Improved, grip, road holding, looks

Complementary Project: Bigger brakes

Big aftermarket wheels and tires seem to be all the rage, and 5-liter Mustangs sport more than their fair share. A nice set of rims and rubber can add a whole new look, and custom-painted Mustangs rarely look right without them. Given the huge selection of replacement rims and tires, it's difficult to suggest what to use on your Mustang, because it's largely personal preference.

The type of Mustang you have, Fox or SN95 version, will determine the type and variety of wheels you can use. The largest-diameter wheels installed on Fox cars from the factory in the early years (1979–1984) were the Michelin TRX rims. They were metric but measured 15.3 inches in diameter.

For 1985, they were replaced by 15x7-inch cast aluminum wheels, which were the largest size carried up until 1990. For 1991, all V-8 Mustangs got bigger, five-spoke 16x7-inch wheels, although to prevent contact between the beefy tires and the inner fenders, Ford enlarged the openings considerably. This enabled 17-inchers to be bolted on for the limited-production Cobra in 1993.

If you own a Fox Mustang, the biggest wheels you can really install without performing modifications to the inner fenders are 16s on the 1979–1990 cars and 18s on the 1991–1993 models. To prevent rubbing, you shouldn't go wider than 9 inches on any Fox car, unless you plan to have the fenders rolled.

One of the most popular aftermarket wheels with 5-liter Mustang owners is the so-called Cobra-R, originally installed on the limited-production 1995 Mustang of the same name. These wheels are available with both four- *(shown)* and five-lug configurations, in different sizes and either regular aluminum or chrome finish.

A budget alternative to shelling out for high-dollar aftermarket rims is to find a set of "10-hole" 15-inch rims originally installed on 1985–1986 GT and 1985–1990 LX Mustangs. These are still cheap and plentiful, and they look really good when polished.

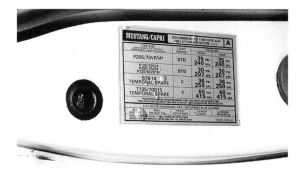

If you aren't sure what size tires your Mustang originally came with, check the original tire pressure sticker (if the car still has it) on the passenger-side door jamb. This is particularly useful in helping you gauge the different sizes that will clear the stock wheel wells.

Besides size, make sure your choice of wheel will fit properly with your particular suspension and steering geometry. Even factory wheels can cause rubbing from misaligned steering and lowering springs, so offset and backspacing are important.

Another thing that will determine your selection is bolt pattern. From the factory, all Fox Mustangs (bar the SVO and Cobra) had four-lug rotors and axles. They were tough as nails, but they restrict wheel choices, because most cars and thus most aftermarket wheels are designed to work with five lugs. This partly explains why the five-lug conversion (Project 25) is so popular on these cars.

On 1994–1995 Mustangs, Ford wisely went with five-lug wheels and much bigger fender openings. In fact, when these cars were new, many people felt that even the optional 17-inch wheels on GT and Cobra models looked too small. Consider installing a set of 18-inchers on these cars since most of them are now in the prime street-machine phase. They really add to the look of the car, even more than with Fox 5-liters.

You can actually go up to 20-inch-diameter wheels on these cars, though on a regularly driven Mustang, such massive rims are expensive and not really practical. They can easily get damaged, and some designs are prone to bending under sustained cornering load. Therefore, they're best reserved for the show field. You can fit rims up to 10 inches wide without problems. Combined with these cars' improved steering geometry, a wide wheel and large footprint will notably improve handling and grip.

Popular Wheel Choices

It's hard to define what causes some wheels to become more popular than others on a particular car, though for 5-liter Mustangs, a few rims seem to stand out. On the 1979–1990 cars, upgrading to the popular 16x7-inch five-spoke "pony" rims is popular, since these wheels are widely available through the aftermarket. Because they were OEM too, they can often be found at swap meets. They were offered in both silver and chrome finish and can spruce up the looks of your older Fox Mustang for relatively little cost. Bigger, 17- or even 18-inch variations of these wheels are available too and are a good choice if you're building a sleeper street machine.

On 1991–1993 5-liters, which came with 16-inch pony rims from the factory, swapping on a set of 17- or 18-inch Cobra R, five-spoke rims (particularly the chromed variety) really gives the car a classy look and works well with the angular styling, whereas many replacement rims do not. These wheels, available from Ford Racing Performance Parts, are available in both four- and five-lug bolt patterns (though the originals as installed on the 1995 R were five-bolt).

Another rim gaining in popularity is the so-called "Bullitt" wheel, a design that pays homage to the old American Racing Torq-Thrust Ds of the 1960s and was installed on the 2001 special-edition Mustang of the same name. These 17-inch rims are available in five-lug configuration only, so if you wish to use them on a Fox Mustang, you'll have to perform the conversion.

For those who like to spend time at the drags, a set of Weld Draglite rims (that fit both four- and five-lug applications) are often considered de rigueur on quarter-mile-prepped 5-liter Mustangs and have become as synonymous with these cars as Torq-Thrust Ds on vintage 1960s muscle cars.

Tires

One of the most important aspects of the 5-liter Mustang (or any car) is choosing the right tires. Size, construction, tread pattern, and speed rating all have a strong influence

107

Tire technology has come a long way since the first Fox Mustang rolled off the assembly line, and there are thousands of choices and tread patterns. BF Goodrich, Yokohama *(shown)*, Nitto, and others make good-quality rubber—all that's limiting is your mind and budget.

Drag radials, such as those from BF Goodrich *(shown mounted on Weld Draglite rims)* are a great idea for moderately modified street/strip 5-liter Mustangs that spend a lot of weekends at drags. They are legal for both street and track.

on how your car rides and sticks to the road. As far as factory tires on 5-liter Mustangs go, it wasn't until 1985 that the V-8 models got their own special tires. From 1985–1990, Ford used Goodyear Eagle GTs with unidirectional Gatorback tread, sized at 225/60VR15. At the time, these were some of the best performance rubber on the market and were derived from the rain tires used in Grand Prix racing during the 1980s. When Ford switched to the bigger, 16x7-inch wheels, they fitted revised Gatorbacks with a lower profile, or aspect ratio: P225/55VR15.

For the 1994 Mustang, Ford again fiddled with tire choices. On GTs, Firestone P235/55ZR16 tires were standard with the regular 16-inch wheels, with Goodyear 255/50ZR17 tires coming with the optional and larger 17-inch rims. When the 1994 Cobra came along, it got the excellent Eagle GS-C tires (which replaced the old Gatorbacks), sized at 245/45ZR17.

All these tires were designed to maximize performance for a fairly reasonable cost while still being able to clear the stock fender wells. Therefore, making note of what your car came with originally really helps when shopping for replacement rubber. If you're unsure, open the passenger door and look at the jamb by the B-pillar. If the Mustang hasn't been painted, the original tire pressure sticker should be in place and will tell you.

Slicks and Drag Radials

Given the popularity of the 5-liter as a quarter-mile (and, increasingly, road-race) warrior, many of these cars will run slicks at the drag strip or circuit. However, if you own a basically stock Mustang, you'll be better off running street tires, because slicks can wreak havoc with the stock rear suspension at launch, bending the control arms and damaging the torque boxes, among other things. Slicks

are best reserved for seriously modified cars. Even though some variants, such as Mickey Thompson Street E/Ts, are DOT approved, *never* drive with them on the street.

BF Goodrich's Drag Radials, introduced about a decade ago, have become popular with owners of street/strip Mustangs. They're a good compromise between street tires and full slicks, enabling weekend racers to put in some respectable times with virtually stock Mustangs. There's even a sanctioned drag class for Mustangs with these tires, and people like Dwayne "Big Daddy" Gutteridge have made the history books by running low 9-second ETs on stock-style suspension and Drag Radials.

Tire Specs

Understanding what tire specs mean is important when purchasing new rubber, especially for high-performance applications. The speed rating, the sixth digit of the alphanumeric sequence, is particularly important for 5-liter Mustangs. Basically, a tire can be identified as follows:

P225/55VR16

P	a tire for a passenger vehicle
225	the width of the tire in millimeters
55	the aspect ratio—the sidewall height divided by the tread width. The lower the aspect ratio, the lower the sidewall profile of the tire.
V	the speed rating (i.e., the maximum speed at which the tire can function safely). In this case, V means good up to 149 mph (240 km/h).
16	the wheel diameter in inches

As a general rule, tires mounted on 5-liter Mustangs should have one of the following speed ratings for safe driving:

H	130 mph (210 km/h)
V	149 mph (240 km/h)
W	168 mph (270 km/h)
Z	149 mph + (240 km/h+)

PROJECT 37 ★   *Moving the Battery to the Trunk*

Time: 5 hours

Tools: Flat-blade and Phillips-head screwdrivers, wrench, torque wrench, sockets

Talent: ★ ★

Applicable years: All

Tab: $200

Parts: Battery relocation kit

Tip: Mount the battery on the right side of the trunk if possible for better weight distribution.

Performance Improvement: Improved weight distribution, handling, better starting

Complementary Project: Ignition upgrade

With the engine mounted almost directly over the front wheels and the vehicle's tendency to understeer if pushed hard through corners, yielding poor traction on all but the driest of pavement, moving weight rearward on a 5-liter Mustang is a great idea. One of the most cost-effective methods is to relocate the battery to the right side of the trunk. Not only does this help redress the balance of weight, it also frees up space in the engine bay, should you wish to install an aftermarket ignition box or hide the underhood wiring for a custom look.

One of the best ways to relocate the battery is to purchase a kit, such as the one from MAD Enterprises. This includes a case for the battery, fasteners and bolts to secure it to the trunk floor, a brace to keep it in place, and special, long positive and negative cables that are routed from the trunk through the floorpan, right to the starter solenoid and motor.

When you perform this task, also consider replacing your battery. The heavy-duty Optima units, with their colorful plastic tops and distinctive spiral cells, provide sealing qualities far greater than most traditional batteries, so they won't leak and contaminate or corrode the inside of the trunk. These batteries are also suitable for high-power engines that place more of a strain on the alternator and electrical system, so they go hand in hand with modified 5-liter Mustangs.

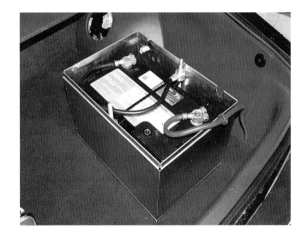

When you're thinking of adding an aftermarket ignition box or installing a supercharger, the battery can get in the way. This is a good time to relocate it to the trunk, which frees up space and improves weight distribution in your nose-heavy Mustang. Mount the battery on the right side of the trunk or hatch for best results.

MISCELLANEOUS

109

Resources

Da Silva Racing
Starting out as a backyard operation, Da Silva Racing has grown to become one of the best and most respected specialty Mustang shops in North America. The friendly, ever-helpful staff live, breathe, sleep, and race 1979-to-present Mustangs and can supply you with just about anything you need for your 5-liter. They also provide complete performance packages and upgrades and have a tech line to answer any questions. Owner Joe Da Silva also races in the hallowed Pro 5.0 ranks and has built some of the quickest and most memorable street and strip Mustangs of recent years. Call 416-847-1500 or visit www.dasilvaracing.com to find out more.

Chilton Repair Manuals
Big and packed with tons of information Chilton manuals usually cover a whole range of vehicles, so they tend to generalize about specific topics and aspects of individual cars and trucks. However, the company does offer two specific Mustang manuals, strangely divided into 1979–1988 and 1989–1993 models, which are worth adding to your collection.

Haynes Workshop Manual
For around $15, it's hard to go wrong with this. Available in two separate volumes—one for 1979–1993 and the other for 1994–2004 models—it covers the basic teardown and rebuild of a late-model Mustang. Although they tend to gloss over some models and repair procedures and cover rebuilding or replacement only for stock vehicles, these manuals still represent good value. They're particularly good for understanding the major components of your Mustang and tackling little, oft-forgotten projects, such as heater replacement and wiring.

Level 10 Transmissions
If you're planning on hot rodding a 5-liter that shifts gears itself from the factory, you'll need the services of an experienced automatic transmission builder. Level 10 has been building and modifying automatics for years and has done thousands of AOD and AOD-E upgrades. If you're looking to get the most from your slushbox-equipped Mustang, give the folks at Level 10 a call at 973-827-1000.

Mustang Enthusiast
This is a fairly new publication that takes aim right at the street-going 1979-to-present Mustang crowd. It brings the latest developments and some of the flashiest show cars in the late-model Mustang world, along with performance trends and motorsports (particularly road racing), in an entertaining format. Unlike several other titles focusing on these cars, *Mustang Enthusiast* features a lot of basic maintenance, restoration tips, and upgrades the rest of us can tackle. It also has restoration articles and historical perspectives on the early Fox cars, which makes it an invaluable resource.

Muscle Mustangs and Fast Fords
The original 5-liter Mustang magazine, *Muscle Mustangs and Fast Fords* has been around for a long time. It focuses mainly on upgrading and modifying your 1979-to-present Mustang, with theory and practical tech articles that cover all budgets and upgrades—from mild to wild. It also provides unrivaled show, drag, and road-race coverage, road tests of the latest factory Mustangs, all the latest news from Ford, features on some of the wildest Ford ponies ever to hit the pavement, and even its own shootout events. These bring together Mustang enthusiasts from across North America (most of whom are *MM&FF* readers), who get the chance to ring their own steeds and see how they perform on the track. For around $5 per issue, it'll be money well spent.

Mustang GT Registry
A huge number of specialist Mustang websites exist, but one of the best is the Mustang GT registry (www.mustanggt.org). It focuses mainly on 1982–1993 GT models and features a comprehensive year-by-year analysis, VIN decoding, some useful links, and a message board, where enthusiasts can post various 1982–1993 GT-related topics. Although you'll often have to sift through a number of posts to get to the real meat on the board, you'll find extremely useful and informative topics rarely found on other Mustang websites.

Mustang Monthly
Founded in 1978, *MM* is one of the longest-running specialty Mustang magazines and has gone through several changes in ownership and content. Although it focuses primarily on 1964 1/2 to 1978 Mustangs, it has some useful restoration and maintenance tips for 1979–1995 owners, including an informative "late-model" tech column.

The Official 1979–93 5.0 Mustang Technical Reference and Performance Handbook, by Al Kirschenbaum (Robert Bentley Publishers)
This is considered the bible of 5-liter Mustang reference material. This paperback contains just about every technical aspect and fact imaginable concerning the 1979–1993 302-engined models. If you can't find it here, you probably can't find it anywhere. This is a must-have for any 1979–1993 5-liter Mustang enthusiast/owner.

5.0 Mustang and Super Fords
Originally a spin-off of *Mustang & Fords* magazine, this title focuses on tuning and modifying 1979-to-present pony cars. Besides showcasing some of the most radical cars around, it focuses on the latest high-tech parts, theory, and practical tech articles and the burgeoning NMRA drag series. It contains useful information for the average 5-liter owner too, including engine swap articles, buying Mustang projects, and a few basic bolt-ons and upgrades.

Latemodel Restoration Supply
This has become a veritable gold mine among Fox and SN95 Mustang enthusiasts. Latemodel Restoration Supply offers a superb and comprehensive line of hard-to-find restoration parts, particularly for 1979–1993 models—and at a perfect time, considering that Ford has discontinued the majority of its OEM stock. From door handles to floorpans, if you need it, LMRS is likely to have it. A bonus is that the list of replacement parts continues to expand, and if they don't have the part you're looking for yet, it'll appear sooner or later. Call 866-50RESTO or visit www.50resto.com.

Mustang Parts Specialties
If you want a new steering rack for your 5.0, a complete rear hatch with glass, an engine, or even an entire car, Mustang Parts Specialties can help you. America's number one late-model Mustang salvage yard has been buying, selling, and parting out damaged ponies for more than a decade and has amassed an unsurpassed inventory of replacement parts and repairable 1983-to-present Mustangs. All parts are usually stripped off acquired vehicles within a couple of days and thoroughly inspected and cataloged. MPS can also help you search for that elusive part if not in stock and will even ship items to your door. They can be reached at 770-867-2644 or at www.stangparts.com.

Texas Mustang Parts
Starting out as a restoration and performance parts source for vintage Mustangs, Texas Mustang Parts has also jumped into the 1979-to-present market with a splash. The company offers a huge variety of performance, customizing, and, increasingly, restoration parts for Fox and SN95 Mustangs. You can obtain parts ranging from high-flow cylinder heads and intakes to replacement fender emblems and the center console latch, all under one roof. Visit www.texasmustang.com or call 800-527-1588.

Dave's Mustang Parts
For a number of years, Dave's has been a popular source for affordable 5-liter Mustang performance upgrades and gained notoriety for supplying Fox owners with complete 5-lug conversion kits. Although now concentrating primarily on supplying brand-new, quality speed parts, the ever helpful staff at Dave's can still provide you with just about anything you need. Call (505) 344-8393 or visit www.daves-mustang-parts.com.

Index

**101 Projects for Your
1964 1/2-1973 Mustang**
ISBN 0-7603-1161-7

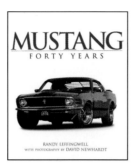

Mustang: Forty Years
ISBN 0-7603-1597-3

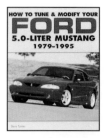

**How to Tune and Modify
Your Ford 5.0-Liter
Mustang 1979-1995**
ISBN 0-7603-0568-4

Mustang 5.0 & 4.6
ISBN 0-7603-0334-7

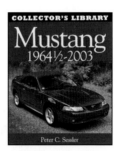

**Mustang 1964 1/2-2003:
Collector's Library**
ISBN 0-7603-1373-3

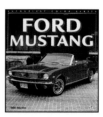

Ford Mustang
ISBN 0-8793-8990-7

**Mustang:
The Original Muscle Car**
ISBN 0-7603-1349-0

How to Paint Your Car
ISBN 0-7603-1583-3

**Ultimate Auto
Detailing Projects**
ISBN 0-7603-1448-9